THE PARENT'S GUIDE TO
COACHING HOCKEY

Richard Zulewski

BETTERWAY BOOKS
CINCINNATI, OHIO

33135

Illustrations by David Seal
Typography by Park Lane Production Services

97 96 95 94   5 4 3 2

Library of Congress Cataloging-in-Publication Data
Zulewski, Richard
    The parent's guide to coaching hockey / by Richard Zulewski.
        p. cm.
    Includes index.
    ISBN 1-55870-308-X
    1. Hockey for children--Coaching. I. Title.
GV848.6.C45Z85 1993
796.962--dc20   93-4792
                                                            CIP

*This book is dedicated to the three people
who most inspire me to work my hardest:
my beautiful wife, Kathleen,
my wonderful son, Thomas, and
my newborn baby daughter, Stephanie.*

Thank you, I love you.

CONTENTS

A TRIBUTE TO …

I'm going to open this book with a brief, well-deserved tribute to a very special man. He was not a great hockey player or a hockey coach. In fact, he never played the game. He was a baseball coach, "just" a Little League baseball coach.

This coach never led his kids astray and never taught his kids anything they or he would regret, ever. He's never had to leave a team in disgrace, never had to apologize for his actions, and never had to explain his motives. He was, and still is, the quintessential role model. With an eventual seven kids and thirteen grandchildren of his own, he started his own team, and coaches his children and his children's children the way he taught his first players. He loves each of them as his own. He's fair, honest, and accepting. He respects his players as human beings and as people.

I could only hope that we as coaches and parents will have just one-tenth the coaching ability of this man. I have met no one with a better coaching skill, coaching style, or coaching demeanor than this man. He taught lessons on the game that couldn't be learned from any book. He taught determination, self esteem, dedication, perseverance, sportsmanship, and fair play. Go right ahead; any positive clichéd attribute that comes to mind applies here. Vince Lombardi was wrong. Winning isn't the only thing. There's so much more to be taught—so much more to be learned—than winning at any cost. This coach knows it, his family knows it, and his players know it. His impact and his message as a coach has shown to be universal. It is lived out in his life and in the lives of his family and his players. His wall is full of trophies and plaques, but just as many of them are for being honored by his team for being a great coach and a great human being as they are for team championships.

I've never had the honor to be coached in baseball by this man, but I have been coached in life by him. Thomas Joseph Christmann. Tom Christmann. To his wife, he's Tom. To me, he's my father-in-law. To my wife and me, he's "dad." To my children, he's "pop." But to the rest of the world, to the youth of yesterday's America, who are today's leaders and tomorrow's role models, he's "Mr. C." God bless you, dad; God bless you, Mr. C. We all love you … and thanks!

INTRODUCTION

Oh, what a sport this game of hockey is—full of excitement, motion, and drama—simultaneously dangerous and fluid. A sport so graceful it appears at times to coax gravity into a temporary respite, if not actually defy it. Blades of steel appear to glide ever so gently over the frozen surface. In one moment hockey gives you inspiration and desire; in the next she cuts you like a razor. Make no mistake about it, hockey is a hazardous and precarious sport. It requires absolute attention and devotion. The men and boys and women and girls who play this game need to focus their energies and concentration totally on it.

Regardless of the ages or sizes of its players, from the most diminutive to the most colossal, a team does not function properly without a coach. The coach is the one constant in junior hockey, by its nature a transitional sport. Players come and go with regularity. Some make it to all the games, others make it to only a few, but the coach is always there. It is the coach who plots the course and sets the bearings for the team. It is the coach to whom the players look for guidance. You as a coach are now a surrogate parent, a teacher, and a sage—a guide, a leader, a tutor, and a guru. These are major responsibilities for anyone to assume, yet all of them are dropped onto the coach's shoulders.

Congratulations, coach, you have just entered the world of sports. Take your responsibilities very seriously, for many people are depending on you. Make it clear to all of your players and to all of their parents from the very beginning, the things you will be taking most seriously; sportsmanship, honesty, fair play, and schoolwork. You will expect good, hard, honest efforts, teamwork, enthusiasm, and a desire to play the game. The one thing you should take the most seriously above all —the one thing I emphasize most vehemently, is to make sure that everyone on the team knows how to *have fun*—and that includes you!

I honestly believe that we are all there to *have fun*! No one would put himself through the pain and agony that the game sometimes becomes if he were not having fun. I make sure that my players and everyone else involved with the team have a good time. Coaches, trainers, and players don't want to come to the rink unless they are there to enjoy themselves. When it stops being fun, maybe it's time to stop playing or coaching this wonderful game.

Don't worry excessively about the mechanics of the game. The skills, wisdom, and coaching abilities develop with time. There will be many opportunities to better your understanding of the game. You'll be bombarded with offers to attend workshops, clinics, and seminars to improve your knowledge of the game as soon as your name gets on the team's roster of the team as its coach, and the roster is turned into USA Hockey (formerly AHAUS), the governing body of amateur hockey. They tell you everything you need to know on *what* to coach and *how* to coach it. What they don't tell you, however, is how to *be* a coach. You've taken the first steps— you have accepted the offer to be the coach and you've purchased this book—so you must care about the kids. Now don't let them down and remember—*have fun*!

Even if you have not chosen to be the official coach for your child's team, as a parent, you want to be as knowledgeable as possible in order to coach your own child in practice. This book will provide you with the necessary information to encourage your child's safe, exciting participation in the sport of hockey.

But first, before we get too deep into the mechanics of the sport, and for better clarification as we get deeper into the book, let's first review the basic classifications or levels of play that there are in ice hockey. They are:

Classification	Age Levels
mighty mite	6 and under
mite	7—9
squirt	10—11 (10—12 for girls)
pee-wee	12—13 (13—15 for girls)
bantam	14—15 (no bantam classification for girls)
midget	16—17 (16—19 for girls)
junior	18—19 (no junior classification for girls)
pro	19 and up

1.

THE SKILL, ART & IMPORTANCE OF SKATING

From a young age, little ones are warned to avoid the ice, avoid stepping on the ice, avoid falling on the ice. Ice hockey directly contradicts all of these warnings. Here is a sport that is played on the ice; requires not only stepping, but running on the ice (on thin blades of steel); and falling on the ice regularly. Logic says that the most natural sports to play are those that involve little to no personal equipment, no special facilities to play on, and no special training to play. The quintessential natural sport using these guidelines would of course be soccer. Ice hockey is the direct opposite of soccer in all of these respects. It is played on a surface that is natural to the environment only in certain extreme locales during select parts of the year, and on a surface we have been trained to avoid. It is played using equipment that covers most of the body from head to foot (and even beyond) making natural movement nearly impossible. Finally, it is a sport that must be learned, developed, cultivated, and bred within the player.

In most other sports, the coach needs to devote little time to developing such basic principles as running. Still, it is generally assumed that children learning "land" sports can naturally propel themselves or run in the manner that is required and necessary. Some fine tuning and intensive training may be required, but the movements are natural. Ice hockey coaches, however, almost always need to develop and cultivate the art of skating not only in the youngsters starting out but throughout all levels of play even up to the National Hockey League level. The ability and aptitude to skate well is the single most important skill that any player can have and every player *must* have, maintain, and hone. The ability to skate skillfully and efficiently is usually the deciding factor between a good player and a great player.

We cannot forget that when a player steps off the ice, he or she unlaces the skates and walks away from the rink in sneakers. The actual time spent on the ice practicing the one skill that is the *most essential* is of short duration, usually only an hour at a time. One hour every couple of days or once a week is just not sufficient time to develop the required skating talents. It is the responsibility of the player and, in the case of the youngest players, the responsibility of the parents to seek out, secure, and utilize as much ice time as possible. This time should be used for worthwhile practice; developing the strong legs and skillful feet necessary to play a masterful game.

SKATES

Without good skates that are properly fitted, all the talent and training in the world are wasted. Skates must feel like natural extensions of the feet for the player. A player cannot worry about his skates and still play an effective game. The feet and skates must act as one unit. Skates that are too big, too old, too sloppy, too tight, or have no support just cannot perform as the proper tools for the job. You would never ask an artist to paint your portrait with a roller brush, that's just not the proper tool. Likewise, never ask your players to go out onto the ice without the proper skates. Improperly fitted skates can also be very dangerous! Please do not allow your child to buy or play in skates three sizes too big with ten pairs of socks worn to take up the excess room. The socks get wet and heavy, they begin to compact due to the sweat and the weight of the child and they lose their "effectiveness" as padding.

I know that skates are very expensive. In fact, they will probably be the most expensive piece of equipment your child owns. But please, for your child's sake, get appropriate skates that fit properly. They do not have to be the professional top-of-the-line model that costs hundreds of dollars and is worn by Walt Watzhisname. But be wary of buying them from the local discount store. Buy a reputable company's product (CCM, Bauer, Micron, Daoust, and Lange are all excellent brands). Besides quality, these companies offer consumer support and warranties. Many of the cheaper skates on the market are made of poor synthetic materials that break down easily and need to be replaced often, provide little support, and begin to hurt the player's feet after only a few minutes of wear. Two or three pairs of cheap skates a season over two or three seasons will cost as much as—if not more than—a single pair of better quality skates that will last several seasons. Take the time to get your player's feet fitted properly by your skating professional at a

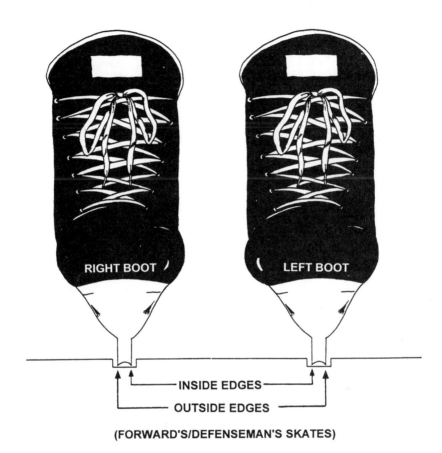

ILLUSTRATION 1-1. *Hollow ground versus flat ground blades.*

professional shop. Visit the store, explain your player's level of skating (and the finances available), and listen to what they have to offer. The salesperson will be happy to show you a complete line of appropriate skates, not just the one or two pairs that the local discount store may carry.

THE MECHANICS OF SKATING

Before we go into what to practice, it is important to know how we are able to actually skate on ice with only two thin blades of steel. It is important that you understand future mention of the inside edges and outside edges of the blades, and see the importance of the part friction plays in skating.

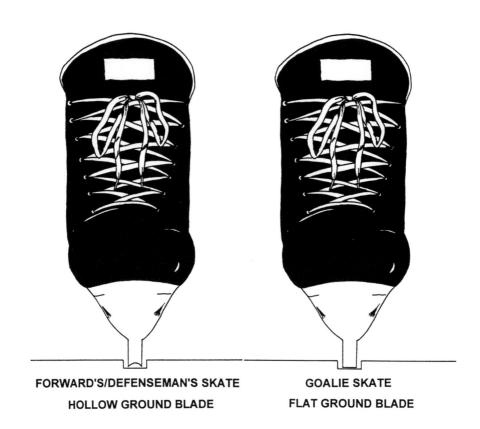

FORWARD'S/DEFENSEMAN'S SKATE   GOALIE SKATE

HOLLOW GROUND BLADE   FLAT GROUND BLADE

ILLUSTRATION 1-2. *Hollow ground versus flat ground blades.*

Refer to Illustration 1-1. If you are standing in your skates on the ice, you have a left and a right skate with a skate blade attached to each. Each blade has two edges: an inside and an outside edge. Hockey blades for forwards and defensemen are "hollow ground." This means that they have a very shallow and minuscule concave cut in the center bottom of the blade surface running the length of the blade that provides for two separate and distinct sharp edges on each skate. These are used to hold the ice and to turn. Without these edges, a skater would not be able to make the sharp turns and quick stops necessary in a game. When a player gets his skates sharpened, the two edges of the blade are being sharpened in order to increase maneuverability.

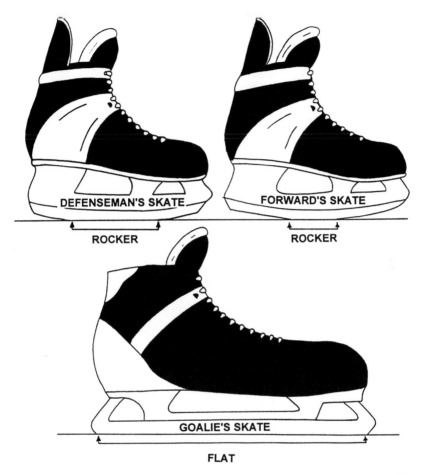

ILLUSTRATION 1-3. *The degree of the rocker cut on the blade will depend on a player's position and skating ability.*

In contrast to the defenseman's and forward's skates, the blade of a goalie's skate is flat ground; that is, it has a flat rather than concave bottom surface. In addition, the blade is much thicker or wider than a forward's blade and has fairly dull edges. The width is needed to increase and maintain stability for the goaltender. Because the goaltender does a lot of up and down movement and generally goes through a wide range of peculiar motions on his skates, the wide blade helps him establish and maintain his balance on the ice. The goaltender uses his skates for a series of lateral sliding movements back and forth across the crease (the area directly in front of the goal defined by a semi-circle). Because his skates are flat and do not have sharp edges, the goaltender is better able to make this type of movement. Because of his bulky pads, the goalie simply cannot turn as adeptly as a forward can, nor does he need the ability to do so. His primary goal is stability. The difference in skate blades reflects this difference in function. (See Illustration 1-2.)

In addition to the different cuts on the skates, different positions and skill levels have different "rocker" cuts. When you look at a hockey blade on the ice surface, the bottom of the blade appears to be resting flat against the ice. It is not. The blade has a rocker cut on the bottom, much like the rockers on a rocking chair, so that only a portion of the blade actually rests on the ice surface. The amount of rocker depends mostly on the individual player. As a player gains more experience and knowledge about his particular skating style, he will often adjust the degree of rocker to suit his own habits and tendencies. The greater the rocker cut, the smaller the amount of steel actually resting on the ice at one time. Generally speaking, forwards have the greatest degree of rocker cut; often only a third of the blade rests on the ice at one time. This allows them the ability to make quick sharp turns and provides very little friction when flying across the ice. Defensemen have about half the blade on the ice at one time for they need greater stability to check opponents (knock or push them off their skates) in the defensive zone. Goaltenders generally have a completely flat blade with no rocker at all. They need maximum stability and full blade on the ice at all times to stop the pucks at all angles and positions. (See Illustration 1-3.)

When you go to the skate shop to select skates, the sales staff will help you choose the correct rocker cut for your youngster. As a rule, the less experienced skaters will require the least rocker cut. Also while you are in the skate shop with the player, ask the salesperson to show you both how to lace the skates properly. Many young skaters lace their skates way too tightly and complain about hurting feet after a few minutes. What do they expect?—no blood is getting to their feet! The skates I wear fit so exactly and so precisely that I lace my skates very loosely for a perfect fit. But this is not for everyone. Each player will have to experiment to find out which lace configuration feels most comfortable. In order to have any chance to find the proper, most comfortable lacing position, the player will have to buy skates that fit correctly from the beginning.

Finally, for those of you curious as to how someone can actually stand up on pieces of metal and glide smoothly across the ice, the answer is really quite simple. As the blade is pressed onto and across the ice surface by the weight of the body moving forward, friction is created. Friction provides heat, and heat melts the thinnest top surface of the ice, causing a "rut" to be formed on the ice surface as the blade moves across it. This rut is very small and will not interfere with skating. It does, however, prevent the blade from sliding sideways. Friction and heat, as they melt the ice surface, cause a thin bead of water to form, but because the ice is maintained at a steady twenty degrees, the water quickly refreezes and fills in the rut. Over the course of a game with a lot of skating action, a lot of ruts and refreezes occur. That is why the ice needs to be resurfaced occasionally with hot water. The excess ice caused by the refreezing water is shaved off flat and a layer of hot water is applied with a large flat "mop" to melt the entire top of the ice surface at once so it refreezes as a flat surface. This is the job of the Zamboni, which all skaters have come to know and appreciate.

PRACTICE

Now let's get down to how and what to practice.

Practice Goals

Stress to your players the importance of having goals of practice. Show them how to practice with a purpose, even if they are practicing alone. These are suggestions that my players have found useful and have resulted in improvements in skating and puckhandling ability. Encourage your players to:

❑ Write down practice objectives on an index card and refer to them periodically throughout the skating session.

❑ Keep notes on progress during practice if possible. Do not rely on memory.

❑ If more than one player is practicing, each can be more objective about the other's skills than he is about his own. One can see the skill areas that the other is working on from the third person perspective and provide the necessary encouragement to continue when the skating gets boring or tiring.

❑ If a non-skater is present, he can sit in the stands and see from a distance the skating skill, style, and speed that is often missed while on the ice. He can shout down directions to change exercises every ten minutes or so.

❑ Use a video camera to tape practice sessions.

❑ After the practice session, review the notes or videotape taken during the period or discuss specifics with the non-skating viewer. It becomes easier to view a session impartially an hour or so after it has ended to check out flaws as well as successes.

❏ Plan ahead for your next practice session.

❏ Keep track of progress and failures.

❏ Increase goals each time out. For example, if you did ten times around the circle with crossovers, next time make it fifteen.

❏ Know your strengths and weaknesses and work from these to strive for improvement.

❏ Improvement is guaranteed by work and practice.

❏ Drill and application will strengthen even the strongest skater.

Practice Without Sticks

Do not let your players practice their skating skills with their sticks in hand. This may be confusing at first, but let me explain. When a player is learning to skate, he will look for every opportunity to prevent himself from falling down onto the ice. This protective tendency can lead to the development of strange skating styles; hunched over, stiff-legged, arms out wide. As a skater improves, his body also becomes more comfortable and more relaxed, and is more adapted to the ice surface. If a skater practices skating while carrying his stick, he will begin to rely on the stick as a crutch. The body will naturally begin to lean on the stick to protect itself from falling. It is easy to begin to use the stick as a pivot point in turns and as a balance pole when in awkward positions. The beginning skater's body will adjust to having this stick *as a crutch* as he skates. This is bad news for several reasons. Not only will the skater be without his stick on occasion—it can often be lost or broken in a game—but he will be unable to hold the stick at the optimal angle for puckhandling if he feels it is a balance pole. Moving the stick into correct position for play will then make it a liability—it will be an extra weight that pulls the player off balance.

In addition, the stick can be dangerous to other players when a skater is practicing new skating skills. The player may be practicing a new maneuver or turn that causes him to fall often. The stick then becomes a dangerous weapon against his own body and the bodies of other skaters. For all of these reasons, your players should leave their sticks at the bench when practicing *skating* skills.

Practice with Equipment

As opposed to the above advice about practicing with the stick, players should always practice while wearing as much of their regular equipment as possible. This may seem contradictory, but it is

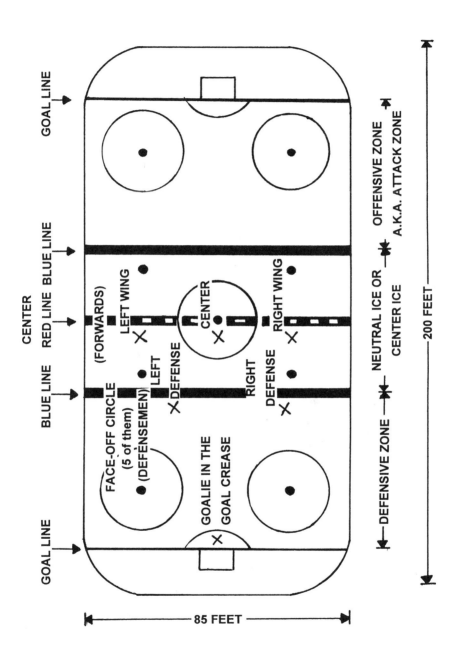

ILLUSTRATION 1-4. *This is the basic layout of the ice with the impor-*
tant marking on it. The diagram also shows the starting locations of the
position players waiting for a face-off.

not. As your players practice, their bodies get used to certain conditions, weights, and positions. Wearing pads and equipment while you skate gives a different feeling from skating in "street clothes." If a player is unaccustomed to the pads and equipment, they can throw her balance off, limit her ease of movement and range of motion, and affect the way she skates and plays. But unlike a stick, the equipment and pads cannot be lost on the ice; they become neither a liability nor a crutch.

The most important reasons to practice with the equipment on are sweat and protection. Sweat helps to break the pads in, especially if they are new. Sweat helps to form the pads better to the player. Finally, sweat weighs a lot! Really. Your players will be surprised (if not shocked) to feel the difference sweat makes. After sixty minutes of hard, intense practice the equipment is soaked with sweat and weighs almost twice what it did when they first put it on. Forwards and defensemen will be carrying around twenty pounds of equipment, while goaltenders are carrying around forty to fifty pounds! Their leg muscles will really begin to feel it. Their bodies will begin to ache ever so slightly from carrying around the extra burden. This is the time that your players will build up stamina and breath support. Encourage them to think about the game situation. Third period, trailing by one goal in the playoffs sometime in the hot month of April. They are sweating like crazy. You call on them to make the final offensive rushes but they can barely get themselves over the boards. They're so tired and weighted down with sweat that they can't even move because they didn't practice with their equipment on and didn't count on sweat being the toughest opponent of all.

There is an even more important reason than stamina to ask your players to practice while wearing their pads and equipment—safety. Although practice is often thought of as an informal time to work on hockey, it really turns out to be the most formal time to practice in the least restrictive environment. What I mean by this is that the players are often "off" their game guard and are concentrating on the skills at hand. As a result, the players are (hopefully) paying close attention to what the coach is saying and how their skills are progressing and may not necessarily be looking out for the odd plays going on in other parts of the rink. Pucks still fly and skates are still sharp in practice—and the ice is just as hard. Even on a public skating rink without pucks and sticks, a beginning or thoughtless skater may whiz by and catch one of your players off guard and down to the ice he'll go. His head can crash resoundingly to the hard ice surface; he may put his hand down to break his fall as other skaters with sharp blades are skating past ... you get the picture. It is always best for safety's sake to practice with the equipment on. At the very least, insist that your players wear their helmets, gloves, and shin guards.

WHAT TO PRACTICE

Just as in a game, there comes a time when all the preparation is over and the show begins. Here are several exercises and practices to help your players become great skaters. (See Illustration 1-4.)

Starts

Essential to every player's game is the ability to get a fast start out of his team's end to begin an offensive attack or to hustle back into the defensive zone to break up a forming play. The basics for practicing this skill are:

RUNNING START

Have your players start from a standing or idle position and lean slightly in the direction they wish to travel, pull up onto their toes, straighten their bodies so they are upright, and begin to "run" on the toes of their skate blades in the desired direction of travel for four or five total steps. The number of steps may vary according to how fast a start is desired and how far they need to go, but five is a good starting point. They should *not* be gliding at this point.

Remember the part about friction? The more of the blade that comes in contact with the ice surface and the longer that contact is sustained, the greater the friction and the more resistance encountered. The object of the fast start is to put the minimum amount of blade possible on the ice surface in order to create the least amount of friction. By running across the ice, the player's body is forced into a position that will allow the momentum of his weight to thrust him forward when he makes the transition from running to skating after a few steps. You must remind them, however, that because there is very little steel on the ice surface, there is very little stability and the player is very vulnerable at this point. A player beginning with a running starts can be easily knocked off balance.

After a few running steps, the player makes the transition into the skating stride. He should thrust his dominant (stronger) foot straight forward and gradually lower it onto the ice surface. It should take another three or four successive steps with each step dropping the blade lower to the ice surface before the entire blade is flush with the ice surface.

Encourage your players to avoid the temptation to put their blades flat on the ice at once. If a player places the entire blade on the ice surface before attaining maximal speed, the blade acts as a brake and slows the player down. Also, the awkward transition from toe skating to full blade skating puts undue strain on the feet and legs. Also, your players should avoid pushing their toes outward as they skate. If the skater pushes his toes outward instead of forward in the direction of travel, the blades put a cross-scraping motion on the ice surface. This increases friction, decreases speed, and puts undue stress on the feet and legs. At first, it will feel more comfortable to the players to push their feet out as that is the direction the legs naturally want to move. Encourage them to push forward toward their target, pointing their toes forward. Remind them that the shortest distance between two points is a straight line. Do not allow that line to waver back and forth.

As both your players and their blades are in full motion now, they should rarely have both blades on the ice at the same time except for the very short transition time between foot exchanges. They are off and flying.

STANDING START

The other type of start is the standing start. This is not a quick start, but a start that leads to a steady pace that allows the player to determine direction of travel as he begins his strides. In this method, executed from a standing full stop or slow circle, the toe of the dominant foot is pointed outward a few inches (up to a full ninety-degree angle depending on which angle is most comfortable to use). The skater digs the first third of this dominant foot's skate blade into the ice as a push-off point while at the same time gliding the other foot along the direction of travel.

Just as with the running start, the entire blade is not placed on the ice at one time; the forward part of the blade is placed first and the transition to the whole blade is made gradually. The skater should keep his weight on the ball of his foot, and use this point as a pivot point around which to travel as he moves. As this foot is pushing forward, the skater brings up the now trailing leg and moves into a full skating stride by thrusting the trailing leg forward and lowering the blade onto the ice toes first. As it will take a few strides to get into full motion and up to full speed, the skater has an excellent opportunity to determine direction at this point. Once he figures out which way to go, he can quickly put full motion and power into the skating strides and take off.

Speed Skating

Really, all skating done in hockey is speed skating. Some speeds may be a little slower or faster than others, but there is very little time for idleness or free skating while on the clock. If your player is starting from the running start, his body will probably be

A running start is the fastest and quickest way to get into the play.

All skating in hockey is really speed skating.
Bear down and get moving!

upright and somewhat stiff. To gain maximum speed while skating, show him how to bend his knees slightly and bend his body at the waist slightly so he is in a very loose, very slight forward crouch. He should alternate swinging his hands and arms with his leg motions for balance and stability.

The next step is to sweep the trailing leg in toward the other leg and then thrust it out forward toward the ice surface for each stride. Remind him not to place the entire blade onto the ice surface yet. (Remember friction?) He should wait until his swinging leg is about twelve to eighteen inches in front of his other leg and then thrust the blade down and across the ice surface pointing in the direction of intended travel. The blade is not placed heel first like walking, but toe first with the front third of the blade contacting the ice surface first and then gliding to the ice. Because of the rocker cut of the blade, the skate will flatten out slightly and the toes will raise up. This movement will be so slight that he probably won't feel it, but it will occur.

If your players are carrying sticks, as in a game, they will not be able to use their hands independently for gaining momentum, but they will be able to use their arms and sticks as a unit to gain speed and balance. As their skating improves and quickens, they can begin to use their arms and legs in a swinging rhythmic motion, coordinating as one complete machine on the move. Proper coordination of all the parts of the body involved in skating—arms, feet, legs, head, hips, and shoulders—should be equal and fluid.

Turns

Turning correctly may be among the hardest skills to learn, practice, and master. It is genuinely a scary prospect to turn when one is first learning to skate. Skaters develop their own styles of turning, and not all of the styles are efficient, correct, or precise; some may even be dangerous. A quick look around the rink will reveal plenty of skaters stopping by crashing into the end boards because they do not know how to turn or are afraid to try to learn. Excellent turning skills are essential to becoming a good skater and player. The ability to turn "on a dime" can make or break the big play and keep a player effective in the play. Poor turning ability can be capitalized on by the opposing players to take a player out of the play. The best and practically the only method of learning to turn is the crossover turn.

CROSSOVER TURN

Basically, the crossover turn is a turn wherein the player picks up the trailing skate and places it in front of the forward skate on the

*Crossovers are really the only way to make a quick turn,
especially near the boards.*

other side of that forward skate while in motion around a turn. The
process is repeated slightly differently for the next stride depending on the direction of the turn. For example, if turning left, the
left skate blade is turned sharply in the direction of the turn. The
body and weight mass with momentum will begin to go in that direction. At this point, the skater is on the left outside edge of his
skate blade and has full weight on that edge alone! The right skate
is then picked up and placed across mid-line and in front of the left
skate and planted down onto the ice so the skater can transfer
weight to that skate and push off with that skate forward. Momentum will keep him moving. Weight is shifted to the right skate,
which is now on the left side of the body.

When balance is reestablished, the trailing skate, in this case
the left skate, is brought up alongside the right skate on the right
skate's left side and planted down a few inches (ten to twelve) in
front of the right skate on the left side of the right skate. Weight is
then shifted back to the left skate and the process is repeated again
until the turn is completed. All of this may take place in less than
one second.

In the case of turning right, the process is identical to turning
left except the skate positioning is reversed. Usually a skater is
more adept at turning one way than the other. It is essential in
learning to practice turning toward both directions. A good idea is

to practice skating around the face-off circles at the ends of the rink in figure eights alternating between the circles. That is, starting at a particular point on the circle near the crease, skate clockwise around one circle completely and then skate to the other circle and skate counter-clockwise around that one. This develops co-ordination, timing, and balance on both the left and right sides.

You can now see how having a quickly executed and precise turn is essential to good skating. Without effective crossover turns, a skater relies on a two-skate gliding turn and does not turn as quickly or as accurately. When a skater is spotted by an opposing coach as not having a good command of this skill, the coach will usually instruct his players to take advantage of this fact and skate to that player's weaker side. The player cannot turn quickly enough in his weak direction to thwart their play or make one of his own.

Stopping

Stopping while skating can be accomplished in a variety of ways. Crashing into someone—like another player—or something —like the boards or net—certainly accomplishes the goal of stopping, but it is hardly efficient and is most certainly dangerous. There are a number of ways to teach your players to stop their forward motion while on skates but the three most common ways are the drag, the snowplow, and the hockey stop.

DRAG STOP

The drag, or glide, stop cannot be used for a quick full stop while traveling at a high speed across the ice. It just does not work. It is more an effort to slow the skater to a stop. The drag is accomplished as follows.

As your player is skating, instruct him to simply lift whichever skate feels most comfortable off the ice slightly and turn it toes out a full eighty to ninety degrees. He will then place the blade flat down onto the ice gently and drag it across the surface perpendicular to his direction of travel. This dragging will begin to scrape off a thin layer of ice as he slows down. Press hard to stop more quickly or press more lightly to slow gradually. This is a very stable maneuver as it keeps both blades on the ice surface, and provides good balance for the beginning player.

The drag is a good procedure for a player to use when cruising about waiting for a play to develop or when the play is across the ice. Make sure that your players practice this with both feet. This should be practiced alternating dragging the left and right feet as alternate stopping procedures. Do not allow them to let one foot become too dominant.

The drag keeps the player poised for a quick start as the weight is on the balls of the feet. Also, because the body is turned slightly at an angle in one direction, it allows him to visually sweep across the ice surface with his eyes and head to see a lot of the action, ready to join in the play.

SNOWPLOW STOP

The snowplow stop is a stopping procedure that is more direct and straightforward both in execution and in physical position. This is not a procedure that can be used when traveling at a quick speed. It can, however, be used to stop when skating at moderate or slow speeds.

When traveling in a forward direction with feet about shoulder width apart, instruct your players to point the toes of the skates inward a few inches and, with the balls of the feet, begin to apply downward pressure to the ice as they glide across the surface. Do not allow them to turn the skates inward more than forty-five degrees. Like the glide stop, they will begin to scrape a thin layer of ice off the surface and can adjust the speed of the stop by regulating downward pressure to the ice. As this is a forward-facing stop and easily regulated by the skater, it is an easy maneuver for beginners to learn and master. It provides a full frontal view of the ice surface. Turns and quick starts can easily be initiated from this stop.

HOCKEY STOP

No hockey player can call himself a complete player unless he has mastered the hockey stop. This is a difficult procedure to learn and perfect but once it is acquired, it is never forgotten. This procedure can best be executed when the skater is traveling at a moderate to high rate of speed. Like all skating exercises, while it will be described here stopping in one direction, it should be practiced in both directions for equal ease of execution.

For the hockey stop, the skater must first determine toward which direction to stop. This in itself is important because this stop does not allow the skater a quick recovery or the quick ability to change direction once the action has been initiated. However, it does allow the player to set himself up for a quick start from the direction of the stop after it is completed. When possible, the skater should stop in a direction that will allow him to see the play and the other players. For this reason, it is important to learn this stop in both directions.

In this stopping action, the skater is significantly off balance during most of the procedure and it helps to have a teammate around who is not going to check the player and send him crashing into the boards. The skater's speed and the desired speed of the

The hockey stop is the quickest and safest way to stop momentum on the ice. Every player should know it.

stop are directly proportionate to how "off-balance" he will be.

Once direction has been determined (to the left for our example), the player will lift the left skate slightly off the ice while weight is on the right skate and pivot his left skate outward sharply to a ninety-degree angle perpendicular to the direction of travel. Using the leg muscles, he will apply hard and abrupt pressure to the outside edge of the left skate and blade down to the ice only. At the same time, the entire body will begin to follow the pivot at the hips in the direction of the left skate and the knees will begin to bend deeply to help the skate dig into the ice. The knee bending also acts as a shock absorber to help take in the pressure of the stop on the legs. The skate, due to sheer momentum, will begin to chatter and glide sharply sideways across the ice surface, raising a large spray of ice crystals. As this procedure is executed, the body itself then begins to move perpendicular to the line of travel.

After the initial "plant" of the left skate, the right skate is lifted off the ice surface, swung around the pivoting body in the direction of the turn and placed smoothly onto the ice surface parallel and close to the left skate. The bending of the knees also assists this movement. The right skate and leg do very little to help the player stop, but they do provide some balance in the stop. If the player tries to use the right leg for stopping at this point, he runs the risk of digging into the ice too deeply with that skate and causing himself to tumble sideways head over skates. Because all of

Skating backward is not only a good thing to know how to do, it's a necessity for keeping your body square to the oncoming play.

the stopping is dependent on the outside edge of one blade, you can see why it is always important to keep the skate blades sharp. Furthermore, because all of the player's weight is precariously balanced on this one razor thin blade, stability is at a minimum. The player can easily be knocked to the ice with little force. When executed properly, the right leg will be in a position to cross over the left leg at the end of the stop to dig in and initiate a quick forward movement if necessary.

This can be a very difficult procedure to master. Teach your players to learn the turns in both directions. They should avoid the temptation to learn the turns in only one direction. Many players feel they are "accomplished" once they have learned to stop and balance in one direction. They see no need to learn or are afraid to try to learn any of the turns in the other direction. The best way to practice is to alternate zigzagging sideboard to sideboard, skating up the rink, turning in opposite directions on each stop. When you reach the top of the rink, turn around and repeat the actions in the reverse direction. By practicing in this manner, the skater learns left and right stops and starts, and turns from the stopped position. The skater can gain just enough speed to make the stop effectively without wearing himself out by skating the length of the ice. The importance of the hockey stop cannot be overestimated. Each of your players should practice it until it is second nature.

Skating Backward

The final basic skating skill that needs to be practiced and learned is the skating backward. Please do not think that skating backward is only for defensemen and goaltenders. Forwards need this ability in order to help out on defense when the team is caught a man down or short. For example, when a teammate has fallen down and is unable to reach the play or a team has lost a player for a penalty. The ability to skate backward makes a good two-way player, and only good two-way players make it to the NHL.

This is actually a very easy skill once the players get the hang of it. Like all skills, this should be practiced early in the skating development period and should be practiced to both directions and on both feet. First have your players select a pivot point on the ice at which to initiate their turns (usually the red line or second blue line is appropriate). Have them begin this maneuver by skating forward from the end boards normally at a decent speed. As they approach the selected point, they should begin to stand more upright than their normal skating crouch and shift all their weight to the ball of their selected pivot foot.

If they will be making a left (clockwise) pivot, the pivot foot will be the left foot. Have the players raise their right skates slightly and keep them up as they swing them backward and across the back of the legs while pivoting on the ball of the other foot. When the turn is completed and their bodies are now moving backward, have them jab the front third of the right blade down to the ice and push off backward or push away from the toe. Because of momentum, the body will continue to move in the original direction of travel except now it will be going backward. In order to keep moving, they must use the first third of the blades of each foot, alternating, and jab and push off the ice away from the toe in the intended direction of travel. With the opposite foot, take large "C" cuts deep in the ice, sweeping the skate from front to back along the ice. That's all there is to it.

The beginning skater will get tangled up and probably will fall a lot. Don't let him get discouraged. Keep practicing the turns. Again, he should turn to the left and then to the right on both left and right feet over and over again up and down the ice. The player can turn back and forth almost five times in one ice length. To turn back to a forward facing direction, reverse the above procedure. When the player wishes to turn, step back with the pivot foot, dig the blade into the ice with the ball of the player's foot and pivot around on the blade swinging the other leg around the first.

To stop while going backward, the only available stop is the reverse snowplow stop. The player can keep his feet either pointed the same direction and at the same angle with toes in and heels out or reversed with toes out and heels in. Just have him press down on the heels of the skates and transfer the pressure to the balls of the feet as he needs quicker stopping ability. From this dead forward-facing stop, he can initiate any skating procedure necessary to get back into the game.

Whew! That's a lot of information about skating. Don't let your players worry. With practice and determination, it will all become second nature to them. In fact it *must* become as much second nature as walking. They cannot concentrate on both their skating and the game at the same time. Putting on a pair of skates and getting out onto the ice should seem as natural as putting on sneakers and running down the block.

FALLING

There is one more matter that must be addressed. Any skater who thinks he will get out onto the ice, learn to skate and to play ice hockey, and never fall, is fooling himself. Like it or not, *everyone*, falls during the course of a game and practice. Skating and falling go hand in hand. Beginning skaters are especially apt to fall as they are learning to skate. So, the best thing to do is to teach your players *how* to fall without hurting themselves in the process.

The most important rule to stress to each player is *never* put an arm out to break a fall. Doing this can easily result in a broken arm. Unlike falling on a street surface where the fall can be offset with the feet, being on the ice in skates and losing balance causes everything to come crashing to the ground at once! If a players puts his arms out, the entire weight of his body plus all his equipment will come crashing down onto that stiffened and outstretched arm. The arm is not designed to take that kind of punishment. When falling on the street, the fall can be controlled and the movement and direction of the fall can be altered by directing the body once it hits. On the slippery ice surface, the arm may go in whichever direction it pleases, many times resulting in very peculiar and painful breaks.

Another reason to stress that a player never put his arm out on a fall is incoming traffic. By putting the arm out as a stiff brace, a player is inviting someone to cut across the arm and trip over it himself and break it. Also, if a player puts his arm out and down, he puts his hand down with fingers spread. With or without hockey gloves on, a large teammate or opponent skating across his hand will do a lot of damage to it and he may even lose some fingers. Remember, those blades can be razor sharp.

The best way to fall is to allow the body to crumple straight down to the ice surface. If your player is wearing shin pads (which you should insist he do whenever he takes the ice), he should try to place most of the burden of the fall onto the pads. He is protected here and the hurt won't affect him at all—or at least very little. Remind players to hold their hands in even if they are falling backward. This is difficult as putting the hands out is a natural tendency. Remind them that they are wearing equipment that is designed to pad them. They should pull their arms in and land on the seat of their pants. Again, they are naturally padded there and they are wearing equipment, so teach them to take advantage of the padding.

In a backward fall, it is also important to pull the upper body forward slightly with the chin tucked down to prevent the head from snapping back. The helmet should be worn at all times. You should *never* allow a player on the ice without his helmet on and securely fastened.

If a player is tripped and falling head first into a dive, he can try to manipulate his body in mid-air to turn slightly so he will land flat on his side. Stress that they avoid landing on their shoulders. The shoulder is a very vulnerable joint that is easily dislocated. Most likely a player will be able to extend his arms out. When he extends his arms out, however, remind him not to use his arms to break his fall but to help push and direct the brunt of the fall so his momentum in falling is pushed along the ice surface and not down onto the arms and chest. Remind your players that since they cannot control the direction of the fall, they might be sliding directly into oncoming traffic. Make sure they remember to keep their hands balled into fists so as not to extend and expose the fingers. Remind them to bring their arms in and tuck them underneath their body or fold them in to protect them as soon as they hit the ice.

As a coach, I have my players rehearse falling to the ice and getting right back up again in practice warm-up. It teaches them to fall correctly and helps them to recover from a fall or hard check by getting right back into the play without losing a lot of precious time. The equipment that a player wears is designed to protect him during the entire game from a whole list of possible injuries. The pads have puck-stopping ability as well as injury-stopping ability. Your players should learn to use their equipment to its fullest advantage—teach them to benefit from the manufacturers' research and from what they paid for the equipment.

ON-ICE TRAINING

Of course, on-ice training is always the most desirable. There is no substitute for the real thing, and it is difficult for your players to acquire enough on-ice training time. The time to practice skating and skating routines is not in a game. The ice time that you are able to block out for team practice is usually so limited, and you usually have such a rigid set of exercises and plays that needs to be covered, there is generally little to no time to practice skating skills. With the exception of the very young players or possibly a "C" or "D" level team, most coaches are able to allot only ten to fifteen minutes of skating drills during the team practice. There is so much to work on that you often need the time to concentrate on team skills and plays. Besides, there comes a point where a player is either a good skater already or he should be seeking out his own ice time to practice skating development.

If you are not the coach, don't be afraid to approach your child's coach and ask his plans regarding the development of skating skills. If you are the coach, have a plan to help aid in this development. A good coach will recognize poorer skaters and help target exercises to improve those weaker skills.

There are many alternatives to acquiring ice time to improve skating skills other than just the few minutes that the team is allotted. First and foremost, what should be understood is if the player is going out onto the ice to work on skating skills, then that is what they should be working on. There should be no horseplay, silly stuff, or tag games. Practice should always be fun, but fun with a purpose. Without a purpose, the valuable ice time can be wasted, the player may develop the wrong attitudes about skating, and may develop poor skating habits. I cannot stress enough that this is *not* to say by any means that skating or practice should not be fun. It should, however, be realized that there is a purpose to what the player is doing out on the ice, and that the coach and player together must work toward their common goal.

If you are not the coach, encourage your child to ask the coach for exercises to help improve his or her weak areas. If you are the coach, encourage your players to ask you specific questions —and be prepared to answer them. A good coach will notice the strengths and weaknesses of each player and will be able to provide specific drills go help the player improve his skating skills. A good team player will be serious about his game skills. If a player shows this level of seriousness and interest, you should be more than glad to work closely with him to help improve his overall hockey and skating skills. Since this book is about coaching hockey and not skating in particular, specific exercises are not included here. There are several excellent books available that cover ice skating thoroughly with specific skill-building exercises. *Ice Skating Basics* by Norman MacLean and any of Laura Stamm's three *Powerskating* books are excellent choices.

Now that the player has a set of skills to work on and has

Face it, it's a fact of hockey life. You will fall many times during a game, so you might as well know how to fall properly.

established his seriousness about working on these skills, just where he finds the extra ice time can be frustrating. Here are some simple hints to share with your team.

Pre- and Post-Practice

Stress the importance of being the first player on the ice and the last player to leave the ice. This is not to "look good" in the coach's eyes, but to provide some uninterrupted practice time on the ice. As a parent, make sure your child is in the locker room early in order to get dressed quickly and be ready to start practice as soon as the Zamboni vacates the ice. There are often five to seven minutes before warm-up begins to work on a specific skill. Encourage all of your players to use that time to their advantage. The same goes for after practice. Of course the kids will be tired and will want to get home. But five to seven minutes of left cross-overs around the circle, of right foot stops, or of reverse turns will make great strides toward improving anyone's game, especially when he is tired or worn. Slow practice after a strong workout will help build up stamina. This kind of dedication helps make a mediocre player good and a good player great.

Public Skating Sessions

These are held nearly every day at very reasonable times at almost every public rink. They are usually family sessions so the whole family can go to the rink and work out. Although many times these sessions can be crowded, they are still held "on the ice." A player can still practice with a purpose. A skater can practice backward skating, especially with quick pivots to both the left and right from front to back and back to front. He can practice hockey stops to both left and right. Even on a crowded rink, it is easy to practice balance by alternating one skate with the other for a length of ice. Younger players can create an enormous edge just by practicing their basic skating skills. Do not overlook the importance of these skills. It is important for the young to learn even the simplest of procedures: how to get on and off the ice with speed and accuracy; how to lace the skates and adjust them on their own as the skating session goes on; even how to let others bump into them without falling down. Public sessions help the player gain familiarity with the ice, with falling down, and with skating on a crowded rink. The more comfortable your young players are with these occurrences, the more ready they will be to work on more advanced skills.

Rent a Rink

It might be possible for a group of ten to twenty players to rent a rink for an hour or two. The available times are often bizarre (like 3:00 a.m.), but *if* the players are old enough, *and* it is not a school night, *and* adult supervision is available, this may be an alternative. As the coach and/or parent, you may also want to place a standing order with the rink operators to let you (or another specific reliable contact person) know if there is ever a canceled session or block of time available during reasonable hours. They will always be happy to rent the ice time—often at a reduced price—rather than let the rink stay empty for an hour or so, especially in the middle of the day.

Other House Leagues

It might be possible to join with another house league that may just be forming. They may have "skating" positions (forward or defense) available that do not conflict with ice times for the primary team. House leagues are usually no more than groups of interested players who form structured teams to compete in semi-formal games. House leagues are fun, great exercise, and great practice opportunities. Players get to be on the ice for some time, and there is the opportunity to work on their skating if the team becomes short of players one night. Remind them to always be prepared! House leagues often meet at rather convenient times, the cost is often not prohibitive, and they can be very friendly and very competitive.

Public Hockey or Open Hockey

Public hockey or open hockey is another option that should not be overlooked. In fact, it may be the last bastion of pick-up hockey in North America today. Granted these sessions are usually held at unusual times, but they are usually somewhat accessible. They may be held from noon to two Monday through Thursday. If a player is off from school that week or even that day for some reason, these are great times to come. These sessions are rarely crowded, always fun, never combative, and they provide a player with an enormous amount of open ice time to work on anything and everything. They are usually cheap, too. You can get two hours of uncrowded ice time for around five dollars. What a bargain! Goaltenders should not overlook this opportunity either. The first four goalies are usually admitted free, and the rink is lucky to get four some days. You may be the only goalie there and you'll get all the work you can handle. Even if you are an inexperienced goaltender, players would rather shoot against a live person than an empty net. You'll see players with varying skill levels. Any player attending these sessions will improve.

Backyard Rinks

Although backyard rinks are more and more unusual, they still exist. Naturally, there are a lot of "ifs" connected to this suggestion. *If* you live in an area that is predominantly below freezing for most of the winter, and *if* you have a large, flat area behind the house, and *if* there is access to a water supply, and *if* you are handy with tools to make some small dasher boards, this may be a feasible arena for practice. Wayne Gretzky learned a lot of his hockey in practice on the backyard rink that his father built. Of course he lived in Canada where the conditions were right, but there are places in the northern United States that fit the description as well. If you think that this may be a viable solution, there are even a few books written that can explain better the procedure for building an outdoor rink. It may take some digging to find the books, but they are out there. Inquire at the local library and employ your local librarian or book shop owner to help you find them. One of the best instruction guides I've seen for building an outdoor rink is Chapter 10 of Jack Falla's book, *Sports Illustrated Hockey*. Falla takes the reader from beginning to end and leaves no questions unanswered.

OFF-ICE TRAINING

Do not be afraid to begin to develop skating skills off ice. Because of the very limited hours that are spent on the ice, it is imperative that an off-ice training regimen be implemented.

Not Weights

This does *not* mean a weight-lifting program. I am opposed to weight-lifting programs for little guys and girls. Young children do not have the muscle foundation necessary to begin arduous work with weights, nor do they have the mental stamina or attitude to work with weights safely and consistently. Young people often lift weights with the mistaken perception that it will build up muscles to make them strong and intimidating. They do not realize that weight training can be used to help develop and refine seldom used muscles or to improve personal discipline. Poorly monitored, the result is too often tragic and dangerous. Young people may develop the wrong muscles or may try to bulk up for the wrong reasons. This off-balance approach to muscle development hinders them in their abilities to perform at both their physical and mental best.

With Ice Skates

Off-ice training can, however, be a lot of other things. First, it is important to emphasize that many off-ice training exercises can and should be done with the skates *on*. Yes, that's right, with the skates *on*! Now before you parents get all upset envisioning cuts and scrapes on your carpets and new vinyl kitchen floors, let me clarify. Put a strip or two of heavy white medical tape over the length of the blades from toe to heel. (Don't forget to remove *all* the tape from the blades before taking to the ice again or a disaster could occur. It is probably a good idea to have the blades sharpened if you are unable to get all the tape residue off the blades.) This protects both the house and the skate blades. The tape also prevents the skater from slipping on waxed surfaces. It also protects against cuts, scrapes, and abrasions that may occur during or because of a fall while doing the drills.

First, the act of wearing skates around the house helps develop balance. Wearing the correctly fitted skates around the house also helps to break the skates in. It develops the necessary "feel" that a player must have for his skates. Skates need to feel like a pair of favorite slippers, but must fit like a skintight glove. The last place to break in skates is in the middle of a game. While wearing the skates to break them in, there are a lot of off-ice games that can be played and enjoyed by players of all ages and skill levels. Here are a few practice drills that will develop balance and foot co-ordination.

☐ Soccer: wearing the skates, kick a soft soccer ball against the wall of the basement. This develops reflexes, skate balance, and maneuverability in skates.

☐ Tennis: use two tennis rackets, one in either hand, and lightly hit a ball against the wall in the basement using alternating rackets in your hands. This develops lateral movement and balance.

☐ Hockey: using a foam rubber puck or a plastic street hockey ball, shoot against a wall from about eight feet away. This of course is the most realistic hockey training and helps develop shooting skills and puckhandling abilities.

☐ Knee drops: while wearing your shin pads (or leg guards in the case of goaltenders) simply drop to your knees and get back up again rapidly. This helps develop vertical movement, stamina, and balance. This is best performed on a soft surface like a rug.

With In-Line Skates

No authoritative work on ice hockey would be complete without addressing in-line skates. In-line skates can be an excellent source of off-season and off-ice training when used properly and used with professional direction. A major advantage of in-line skates is that they are an excellent device for off-season conditioning such as leg musculature development, stamina and endurance, and balance and quickness. In addition, a player can improve skating techniques taking all the time that is needed. Because there is no real limit to parking lot or street time, they can be utilized for improvement for as many hours as a player is willing to work on his game.

There are, however, some disadvantages to in-line skates as training tools. The skates are still fairly expensive. In-line skates should fit as precisely as the hockey skates. For this reason, a player should not borrow other's skates. The expense of two pairs of skates, one for on the ice and one for off the ice is a disadvantage to many parents.

Another disadvantage is the friction created on street surfaces is not translatable to the slippery surface of the ice. A player can obtain a false sense of security and mastery with in-line skates that will quickly be dispelled on his taking the ice. Also, the muscle movements necessary for many maneuvers on the ice are simply not duplicated by the in-line skates. Because in-line wheels are wider than the blades of hockey skates, a player may feel he can relax in many in-line maneuvers that would land him in a fall on the ice.

In addition, in-line skating is not limited to a specific "rink." This has the advantage of providing more opportunity for practice, but the disadvantage of decreased adult supervision. The risk of injury, therefore, is increased. If you do use in-line skates as training tools, please stress the importance of protective equipment. At the very least, you should require your children to wear helmets and knee pads.

All things considered, the use of in-line skates is here to stay and this fact must be weighed when discussing off-ice conditioning. When skating on in-line skates, a skater is using many of the same muscles used for ice hockey. Skating with in-line skates builds stamina, endurance, and breath support. This makes in-line skating an excellent choice for getting in shape for the season and then staying in shape for the next season.

EXERCISES

When practicing with in-line skates, your players should have a specific plan of action for practicing certain moves, exercising specific muscles, and working on specific weaknesses. Remember to warm-up before beginning any exercise routine. Here are some specific exercises to help your players improve their hockey muscles.

- ❏ Deep knee bends: on a non-rolling surface such as carpeting or grass, stand with your arms straight in front of you at shoulder height, bend your knees and ankles. Keeping your back straight, lower the hips to your heels and come back up slowly. Repeat several times.

- ❏ Balancing: on a non-rolling surface, stand straight and square. Move one leg straight up forward to a forty-five degree angle, then slowly circle the leg out and around the side of the body to the back and then bring the leg in again. Repeat five times for each leg. This exercise can also be performed while rolling once balance is improved.

- ❏ Crossovers: using string and chalk, draw a large round circle with a radius of at least fifteen feet on a parking lot and practice crossovers around the circle, alternating directions.

- ❏ Sprints: sprint all-out for twenty to thirty seconds and then rest by leisure skating or coasting for the next minute. Repeat.

❑ Uphills: look for an easy uphill street or parking lot. To begin with, do not choose a grade greater than ten to fifteen degrees or a grade that would take longer than ten to fifteen seconds to climb. Sprint straight up the hill to the top and then turn around and coast down. Make sure you know how to stop before coming down the hill.

For specific information on the use of in-line skates, see *The Complete Guide & Resource to In-Line Skating* by Stephen Christopher Joyner (Betterway Books, Cincinnati OH).

At this point, I think it is necessary to interject a word of caution. Let none of us forget the purpose of the game. No matter how intense things may get, no matter how frustrating skating may become, regardless of who wins and who loses, the bottom line, the cardinal rule is this: *have fun*! Never lose sight of this. As a coach, I stress this to the players over and over again—*have fun*! Do not get this confused with not taking the game seriously. It is a very serious game that can be dangerous when not played with full concentration. I stress to my players that hockey is a serious sport and that everyone involved in it must take his duties, responsibilities, and roles very seriously. But don't ever let it get to the point where it is just not fun anymore—either for you or for your players. If that becomes the case, walk away. If it becomes tedious, boring, tiresome, and monotonous, just walk away. In nearly every interview I have read that quizzes a professional player about retirement, there is a response something along the lines that when it stops being fun, the athlete will retire. Please keep that in mind and stress it to your players.

Coaches, parents, and team and league officials must present a unified front to young players about the policies of the league. Every adult involved should know, understand, and abide by these policies. Children will know if a rift exists among the "adults," and will unintentionally pry themselves into the middle of it. Do not let this happen. If you are dedicated to the kids and to having fun; rifts will not occur. Remind the kids to have fun; they will sometimes take everything *too* seriously. The last two words I say to my players just before they take the ice are "Have fun" and the first thing I ask them after the game is, "Did you have fun today?" It makes more of a difference than you might think.

Armed with this section alone, you can get your players onto the ice and never want for more things to practice. But we need to know now what to do with our newfound skills. How do you put them to optimal use in practice and games situations? Regardless of what comes next, *keep practicing*!

2.

BASIC INDIVIDUAL SKILLS

STICK SKILLS

Regardless of a player's age, skill level, salary, or degree of fun derived from the game of hockey, all players are connected by several common threads. These common threads are basic skills and the stick used to implement them.

The reason we discuss the stick here is that proper stick procedures are required to implement the skills covered in this chapter. It is what makes the game of hockey unique. Without a stick, hockey would just be soccer on ice. The stick is considered one of the two most personal and prized possessions of any hockey player —skates being the other. Players will spend hours whittling and fiddling with their sticks until the sticks are "just perfect", and then will change to another stick after a few shifts into the game for whatever reason. Many players feel that, as the skates are an extension of their feet, the stick is an extension of their arms. The player and stick must act as one on the ice, not as separate parts.

It is not only a coach's job to instruct players in the skills and plays of the game of hockey, but also to see that their equipment is properly sized, fitted, etc. Parents who are not familiar with the sport of hockey cannot be expected to be authorities on it nor can their children. It is unlikely that you will find hockey equipment specialists in the local discount chain store either. Certainly hockey pro shops offer excellent advice, but the staff is often too busy fitting skates to little feet to advise on sticks. That leaves the job back in your hands as the coach or parent.

The length of a player's stick is essential. It must match the size and skills of the player.

STICK LENGTH

The proper way to measure for the correct length of a stick for a player is quite simple. The player should be wearing the skates he would wear in a game. With the player standing upright, have him hold the stick with the bottom front point of the blade touching the ground directly in front of him about eight inches out with the shaft of the stick vertical. The correct length of the stick should be to the point of the player's chin while he is standing erect. If the shaft is longer than this, you can use a hacksaw to cut off the excess. If it is shorter, he should get a longer stick.

You may be wondering what difference it makes if a stick is too long or too short for a player. You may think that two or three inches won't hurt anyone. What problems could be caused? Well, here's the reason we are concerned about stick length. If the stick is too long and the player is in his normal game position, slightly crouched leaning on the stick waiting for a pass, just the heel of the stick blade is resting on the surface of the ice. The toe of the blade is up in the air and the longer the stick, the higher the toe. If the toe is up, then the player is not in a position to receive a pass, take a shot, or make a play. The puck may skip under the blade when the player is receiving the puck. When the player is taking a shot, the blade may miss the puck altogether and the stick may bounce off the ice over the puck because of excess shaft length. When making a pass, the full force of the pass is not transferred to the puck and it may go weakly onto the stick of an opposing player.

If the stick is too short, the problems above are directly reversed. The player is leaning on the toe of the blade with the heel up. He may try to pass, shoot, or receive a pass with the toe of the blade instead of with the entire length of the blade. When hitting off the toe of the blade, the stick twists in the player's hand and the direction of the puck is unpredictable. There is too large a margin for error.

If the player is using the new aluminum shafts which are *very* expensive, you may want to think twice about cutting the shaft. The advent of aluminum shafts is a godsend to the professional player who needs strict consistency in shaft flexibility and torque, and who does not have the time to test all his sticks. But because young players lack the strength to put the flexibility of the wooden shafts to the test in game situations, it is very unlikely that they benefit that much from the aluminum shafts. The player would probably better benefit from using wooden shafts again. The wooden shafts are also slightly lighter in weight for the younger players so they are not carrying unnecessary extra ounces.

As a player grows stronger and smarter about his skills, he may come to appreciate a different length of stick better suited to his individual style of play. A tall defenseman with long arms may want to use a stick that is a little longer than normal. With the combination of his arm length and the stick, he may have the ability to cover twice the ice surface that the average defenseman covers. Conversely, a short wiry forward may want a shorter stick in order to get in and out of traffic jams with the puck without getting tangled up with a big stick. But these fine-tuning decisions are for the pros or at least for older players who have more experience. For the just-starting-out player, stick to stick basics.

TAPING THE STICK

Another important aspect of using the stick is the taping of the stick blade and the handle. Contrary to what some people may think, the tape is a very important part of the stick. Taping the blade increases the puck "control-ability." the tape allows the player carrying or receiving the puck better control as the puck does not slide off the blade. I even know a coach who insists that all his players tape their sticks with black cloth electrical tape—not white medical tape—in order to "hide" the puck on the blade.

The tape on the end of the shaft, or the butt end, gives the player a sticky wide handle to help control the stick. This hold also helps prevent losing the stick when the player has his arms outstretched

Now this is a properly taped stick for a young player. Not too much to weigh it down, but just enough to allow good control of the puck.

As a coach, I feel it is important not to let the players go overboard in taping sticks. Many young players take a perfectly good light stick and turn it into a sledge hammer by weighing it down with rolls and rolls of expensive tape. The coach should illustrate proper taping at one of the earliest meetings. In addition, he should quickly inspect all of his players' sticks before practices to make sure that they are proper to use, "legal" to play with, and not dangerous to have out on the ice because of breaks or splinters.

A properly taped stick has one continuous strand of tape wrapped around it. The tape should overlap just at its edges to create vertical ridges on the blade for better puck control. The tape should start about one inch from the front toe of the blade and continue no further than about one inch from the heel of the blade. Many players may want less tape and that is fine. Don't let players put rolls and rolls of tape on a stick. This just adds weight and has no beneficial effect.

HOLDING THE STICK

Many young players today begin playing hockey holding the stick the wrong way. Mom or dad may buy them a stick from a flea market or toy store with no regard to hand dominance, or the players may join in with a bunch of other kids who have extra sticks and they begin to develop their shooting and puckhandling skills to fit the sticks instead of their sticks fitting them.

Hand Dominance

The correct way to hold a stick is for the player's dominant or stronger hand—usually (but not always) the hand with which he writes—on the top end of the stick near the butt end and the weaker hand halfway down on the shaft. The player needs the stronger hand on top to physically transfer the force of the shot from the arm muscles to the puck, using the non-dominant hand as a stick pivot. That is, the lower hand is used more for direction while the upper hand is used for power.

This is true for all shots except maybe the slapshot where power is needed from the lower hand as well. This is why the slap-shot is considered the hardest shot to perfect in hockey. The player must have power in both hands and be able to transfer the power equally and simultaneously to the puck. In other shots, the player must forgo the tendency to use the lower hand for the power. This causes confusion in hand dominance and does not help the player develop his game. The pattern must be established early in the career and exercised daily so it becomes second nature. Just as in skating, the player cannot be worrying or concentrating on basic stick-handling skills when he should be concentrating on the game.

Grip

The grip in holding the stick is a natural gripping motion, similar to (but not exactly the same as) holding a baseball bat. When holding a bat, we turn the fingers around the shaft and enclose the shaft within the palm. It is impossible to grasp a hockey stick in this way while wearing hockey gloves. Hockey gloves do not allow the fingers to bend completely around the shaft of the stick. The hand in the hockey glove must hold the shaft as a claw of a machine might grasp something between two "fingers." The stick is held with squeezing pressure as the thumb attempts to oppose the fingers. This is another reason to practice wearing equipment. It is a totally different feel than when not wearing any hand protection. Shot energy is transferred differently then, through the palms of the hands and not through the fingers. Encourage your players to wear their gloves whenever they practice stick-handling and puck-shooting skills, even while off ice.

SKATING WITH THE PUCK

Now that the player has basic stick and grip knowledge, let's help him put it to work. Moving the puck from one end of the ice to the other is the most basic element of hockey. By no means, however, is it the easiest. The puck should be advanced up the ice while it is in front of the skater. Many young players will either drag the puck up beside them as they skate or they will kick it along. This is *not* sound hockey! The good player moves the puck in front of him as he moves up the ice by using the toe of the blade and the first inch or so of both sides of the stick blade to push and maneuver the puck ahead of him. Once he is more comfortable with puckhandling, he may even use only the upper hand.

When in control of the puck, a good player never lets the puck get more than a few feet in front of him at any time unless there is plenty of open ice between him and the goal. Only then will he push ahead (shovel) the puck ahead more quickly a few extra feet at a time. Moving the puck ahead helps to gain speed while skating. Without having to worry about the puck, the skater can push harder with his legs to gain acceleration.

In order to skate forward with the puck from a standing stopped position, the player should shovel—not shoot—the puck directly in front of him with either the forehand or the backhand in the intended direction of travel for a few feet, ten feet at the most. The skate will break into his skating stride directly toward the puck and not toward his target. He must gain control of the puck first with the front tip of the stick blade. As the skater approaches the puck, he will push it along in front of him. Once he has control of the puck, he can adjust the direction toward the goal.

Encourage your players not to worry if the puck goes a little off. As they skate with the puck in this manner, they will be controlling the puck and stick with one dominant hand and one steering hand. The blade of the stick will probably have some curvature to it. Assuming a right-handed shot the blade will be curved from right to left. If the puck begins to drift off to the left, the player will use the first one or two inches of the back of the stick, or in this case the right side of the blade, to push the puck ahead of him. If he is beginning to lose the puck off to the right, he should use the first one or two inches of the front or left side of the blade to push the puck along. For a left-handed shot, reverse the above. The player should concentrate on keeping the puck ahead of him. Sound fundamental hockey makes a poor player good and a good player great. Encourage your players to practice skating the length of the ice practicing just this fundamental skill.

Once your players have mastered moving the puck across the ice and are comfortable with the skill of stick-handling, make their job a little harder. Place a couple of orange safety cones on the ice about twenty or thirty feet apart and have your players skate in a crisscross pattern through the cones while stick-handling the puck. In order to skate through the cones, they are forced to change their skating direction. There is a law in physics that directly ap-

Controlling the puck on a breakaway is difficult to do, but never skate with your head down! This little guy is setting himself up for a crushing check at the blue line.

plies to many phases of hockey. That law states that a body in motion tends to stay in motion unless acted upon otherwise. The puck will want to go in the direction you initially sent it. As you are skating and turning, you must either corral the puck in the turn and take it with you, or you must change the direction of the puck and send it to meet you as you complete the turn. Either way will work. As a coach, I prefer to have a player take the puck with him in the turn. The longer the player is in possession of the puck, the better he can control it. When a skater relinquishes possession of the puck, even for a split second, an opposing player is given the opportunity to strip the puckhandler of the puck.

Encourage your players to concentrate on keeping the puck with them as they skate through or around the cones. As their skill levels improve, you can widen the separation of the cones laterally and shorten the distance between them, causing sharper turns and the necessity to hone finer skills.

After your players have fully established their ability to control the puck under the above circumstances, have them try it again without looking at the puck. That's what it takes to be good. Each player should develop a "feel" for the puck and an intuitive notion of the puck's location at his feet and on his blade at all times. Of course he can glance down occasionally to make sure he's got the puck, but it is essential that he learn to move around on the ice with the puck without keeping his head down. Hockey is a game of hitting and checking. Every player gets hit now and again. But a player will get crushed every time if he is skating up the ice stick-handling the puck with his head down. Opponents know when they see this weakness the player will be too busy concentrating on the puck to notice opposing players coming at him. It is dangerous to attempt to carry the puck through traffic with the head down. Another reason to practice with heads up is to allow them to see what is happening on the ice in front of them. Make sure that they practice puckhandling skills with their heads and eyes up so that they look at the players on the ice. Only by looking at the action as it develops can they make intelligent decisions about where to skate, to whom to pass, or when or where to shoot.

Skating backward with the puck is very similar to skating forward with the puck—only it is easier. First, because it is difficult to travel fast while going backward, there is more time to control the puck. The player cannot overskate the puck, kick the puck, or push the puck too far ahead while he is skating backward. Second, regardless of which side (left-hand or right-hand) shot the player is, the curve of the blade acts as a natural cradle to pull the puck back toward him as he skates. Third, players just don't skate backward with the puck too often in the game unless they are very good defensemen or very good defensive forwards, and even then they will only skate with it for a few seconds.

Don't overlook this necessary basic skill when working with your players. Ensure that they know how to execute it and when to use it. It is used most often in defensive situations when the puck carrier is forced to pull away from an opponent as he is being pressured. It is unlikely that your beginning players will find themselves in this position. In the outside event that a player finds himself in this predicament with no other way out, suggest that he immediately shoot the puck quickly out of the zone using a high lofting shot (dump the puck) and ice it to stop play. If the defenseman is a skilled player, he may attempt to backskate the puck deep into the zone to relieve immediate pressure and then escape the zone using one of the defensive escape maneuvers discussed in the chapter on position play.

PASSING THE PUCK

Only the most gifted of professional players can advance the puck the length of the ice without the need to pass it. The multitude of the rest of us must learn sooner or later that they have to pass the puck to someone. They learn early in their careers that a

Being able to make and receive a pass on the backhand is a great skill to master. Practice it regularly.

scoring point is a point no matter if it is a goal or an assist. Some players make their living being great play makers and not great goal scorers. The ability to make an excellent pass is a rare art today even in the NHL. Too many young players hog the puck looking for glory. The pass is the most effective method of setting up a scoring opportunity. It is a picture of beauty to watch a fine pass thread itself through a needle of players to the open man next to the net for the goal. But we know that the puck didn't shoot itself; it needed a lot of help to get there. There was a player on the starting end of that pass who created the goal out of nothing. Make sure that all of your players realize the importance of developing the talent to make the assisting pass.

There are two ways any player can pass the puck—forehand and backhand—and three types of passes that can be made—the shovel pass, the flip pass, and the lift pass. From either the backhand or forehand, the procedure to execute each pass is basically the same. Before the pass is executed, the passing player must determine the direction of the pass and view all potential obstacles. Once this split second survey is completed by the player, the puck is sent on its way. How it is sent is important. The position of the puck on the blade will determine if the puck will travel along the ice surface with the shovel pass, just skim the ice surface and jump over a few sticks with the flip pass, or be elevated significantly off the ice surface to reach its destination with the lift pass.

The Shovel Pass

By leaving the puck on the ice surface, the pass will be slower due to friction. It is easier to control the direction of the pass, but the puck is more apt to be sent off course as it hits flaws in the surface of the ice as it travels. In addition, the intended direction of the pass is more easily read by both the receiver and the defenders. This pass is performed with the puck sitting snugly against the inside curve of the blade toward the heel of the blade where the shaft meets it. We refer to this as the back third of the blade. With the stick gripped in the natural manner, pull back sharply on the butt end of the shaft while using the lower hand on the shaft as a pivot point, and give the puck a sharp push. The keys to this pass are to use very little follow-through and to turn the stick blade flat and parallel to the ice surface. Both keep the puck on the ice. (For a backhand pass, the upper hand is pushed away from the passer.) The amount of energy you need to convey to the puck is in direct relation to the distance the puck has to travel. A long cross-ice pass requires a lot of force for the puck to reach another player on the "tape" (directly on his blade) while he is skating quickly. A short pass may require just a little shove. There is little to no follow-through after the puck has left the blade and the blade is "cupped" downward—that is the lower hand that holds the stick is rolled at the wrist over the stick shaft while holding it. This action turns the blade face down toward the ice. The follow-through is how high the passer lifts the stick off the ice after the puck has left the blade of the stick. The lack of follow-through and the pushing action is what keeps the puck on the ice rather than in the air.

The Flip Pass

This pass is used in a situation where the passer determines that there are several stick blades or skates (of either or both teams) close to the passer in the direction of the pass that may unnecessarily interrupt the flow of the pass. This pass flips the puck over the extended stick blades to land flat on the ice still traveling in the intended direction. The puck should flip about a foot to a foot and a half off the ice surface for just a few feet, maybe six to ten before resuming its surface travel toward the receiver of the pass. The keys to this pass are keeping the puck both flat and moving. Using this pass in the wrong situation, like trying to pass too far, may put the puck directly on the blade of an opponent.

To execute this pass, the puck is cradled in the middle third of the curve of the stick blade. The hands are held in normal position on the stick. The lower hand does equal work with the upper hand in this pass; the lower hand turns, wrist up quickly and sharply while gripping the shaft as the upper hand pulls back (or pushes in a backhand) causing the blade of the stick to scoop the puck slightly into the air. Follow-through is important here. The passer needs a medium stick lift of about a foot to two feet off the ice surface. The higher the follow-through, the higher the puck will go. Do not go higher than two feet. Any higher and the stick blade pulls the puck edge down and starts it in a reverse rotation which flips it. If the puck flips through the air, it may land on its edge and bounce every which way with no control, ruining the pass.

When performed properly, the puck will move forward in a flat spin about eighteen inches off the ice surface. It will then land flat and continue on toward its target with little interruption.

The Lift Pass

The lift pass is executed in the same manner as the flip pass but with the following differences. The puck is cradled in the first third or near the tip of the stick blade. More energy and power are exerted onto the puck, with the upper hand producing most of the power and the lower hand producing a hard, flicking motion. In the backhand, the lower hand will pull the stick shaft down toward the ice then outward from the body in a scooping motion with the back of the blade in the direction you want the puck to travel. (Notice how with the three passes, the power has shifted from the top hand to equal power with both and finally to the lower hand power.)

The last difference is the follow-through. The lift pass has greater follow-through with a pronounced lower wrist and stick blade turn and higher movement off the ice surface. The stick may be lifted up to shoulder level or beyond to get enough power and height behind it. Just be careful where or at whom you raise that stick. This power causes the puck to be lifted high into the air— usually above the heads of all the players. That's why this pass is great to clear the zone and to fast break to a teammate down the ice from your defensive zone. Opposing players cannot intercept it and direction in the air cannot be changed once it is initiated. But remember the physics law. As the puck is traveling through the air, it is flipping end over end. As it lands, it is likely it will land on an edge and bounce wildly unless it is gliding flat. There is no telling where or to whom it may bounce. This pass is used as either a clearing pass or a desperation pass; rarely as a pass to set up a goal.

Passing Drills

It is always best to practice passing skills with a partner. One good drill is to start out a few feet apart at center ice and complete a series of passes—about ten. After each series, each player steps back one step. Repeat the drill as above and keep doing it until you back into the boards. Then turn to your backhand and work your way inward toward center ice and each other.

Another great passing drill for a team to play is keep away. With the team equally divided into two groups and the players spread out around the ice, each set of players is assigned a zone to work in. One team starts by passing the puck to another teammate. The object is to keep the puck moving between members of your group and to keep it away from any member of the other group. Each time the pass is completed, that team scores a point. Try to see how long a string of complete passes can be made by any team.

Another very important skill to master in passing is "leading the skater." An inexperienced player will pass the puck behind the moving receiver. Common sense will tell you that if you pass a puck to a moving player across the ice, by the time the puck reaches his original location, he is no longer there to receive it. The passer must "lead" the skater by from a few feet to several yards so that the puck and the skater will reach a certain point on the ice at the same time. This is an easy skill to practice but a hard one to master. Again, you need two skaters; one passer with an ample supply of pucks and a receiver. From the end boards with both skaters standing on the goal line on opposite sides of the net, the passer yells "Go" and the skater breaks towards center ice. The passer passes the puck to a preselected location, usually the first blue line and not to the skater. It is the passer's responsibility to make sure that the two—puck and skater—arrive at that location together, so the passer must use judgment, skill, and power to perform this drill accurately. It is a fun exercise and one that builds a lot of confidence in the players while building a very important skill.

Receiving the pass is just as important as making the pass. To receive the pass, the passer stands sideways with the curve of the blade facing the passer and puts the stick blade flat onto the ice. He should hold the stick loosely in his natural position. When the puck hits his stick and he is holding it stiffly, the puck will simply bounce off the blade as it would have if it bounced off the stiff end boards. If the stick is held loosely and slightly forward on the ice (the blade should be about a foot ahead of his skates), in your stance, the player is acting as a shock absorber taking in the brunt of the force of the pass with his hands and arms. As the puck hits the stick (he may have to reach or move a little to get the puck) the player should immediately pull the stick back slightly while "cradling" the puck on the tape. If the puck is bouncing or is wobbly, you may have to settle it a little by hitting down on the top of the puck with your blade. To receive the puck on the backhand, it is the same procedure but there is not the cradle of the curve of the blade to help you. In this case, try to receive the pass on the back third of the blade where it is now flat. There is less chance of deflection at this point of the blade. You are now in a position to make another pass, take a shot, or take off with the puck.

SHOOTING THE PUCK

There have been many goals scored in the NHL and throughout all of hockey where the player never did shoot the puck toward the net. The puck has bounced in off defenders; defenders have put the puck into their own net; goalies have misplayed zone clears headed toward them. There may actually have been a game or two won without shooting the puck into the net, but it is very rare. The essence of the game is to carry the puck down the ice and shoot it into the opposing team's goal. Every player needs to know how to shoot the puck. It is a basic skill that goes hand in hand with skating, holding the stick, and passing the puck.

There are four basic shots a player can take. They are the slide shot, the wrist shot, the snapshot, and the slapshot. Each shot from first to last is progressively more difficult to perform and master, each is a progressively stronger or harder shot at the goal, and each is gradually less accurate in its delivery.

The Slide Shot

In its purest form, the slide shot is simply a directed pass made toward the goal. It is performed and executed exactly as a shovel pass would be; in fact it is sometimes called a shovel shot. It is a finesse shot that is used in situations where a "feather" touch is needed. There may be times when the goaltender is going down as the puck carrier approaches. The shooter may see an opening just under the outstretched leg pad. Since a slapshot is hard to control, a snapshot would take too long to get off, and a wrist shot may travel too far off the ground, the slide shot is the logical choice.

The slide shot can be produced with any part of the stick blade. The shooter pushes the puck along and slides it toward the opening of the goal with as much strength as necessary to get the puck across the goal line and into the net. A lot of goals are scored in this manner, but not a lot of young players take advantage of it. They see the flash of the big booming slapshots of the pros and want to look just like them. In their weak efforts to get the shot off, unlike the pros, they fail miserably. The only basic problem with this shot is that not enough players use it. It is such an easy shot to learn and master that it should be the very first shot the beginning player is taught.

The Wrist Shot

The wrist shot is a very quick and accurate shot that gets the puck off the ice surface in a hurry. It is used to carry the puck over fallen defenders, outstretched pads, or downed goalies to reach upper sections and distant pieces of the net quickly before the holes are plugged. It is performed exactly like the flip pass but with considerably more energy transferred to the puck. The follow-through will dictate the height that the puck achieves in flight. The more follow-through, the higher the line of travel. This is generally an easy shot to try out but a very difficult shot to master. The "bread and butter" of this shot is accuracy. Good players can literally place a three by one inch high puck inside a four by two inch opening from thirty feet away! The downfall of many players in making this shot is twofold. Most players either do not have the strength to make the shot work or they do not have the accuracy to place the puck within the net.

Players overestimate their arm strength and their ability to get a puck to travel the complete distance to the net with the necessary force to put the puck in it. To be effective, the shot should be lightning fast so the defenders do not have time to stop it. Often, the puck will begin to falter in flight and never reach its destination. A young player should build and maintain strong arm and wrist muscles through consistent practice, not weight training. Practice and the resulting strength will provide the blazing speed. Players should practice with gloves on and with a regulation puck, especially if they are practicing off the ice. I've seen many players practice with lighter plastic pucks or balls, and then they fail miserably when it comes to shooting the heavy rubber hockey puck. They just don't have the arm strength and stamina to make the shot successfully.

Even if they have the strength, most players lack the accuracy. They often fail to look where they are shooting and just flail the puck toward the net, hoping for a deflection when a direct shot is called for. They keep their heads down while shooting or even close their eyes after they think the puck is on target! We'll discuss accuracy problems later in the chapter, but until then, a player can practice just shooting the rubber puck against a specific spot on a brick wall over and over again.

Most goals are scored with a sharp and accurate wrist shot. Notice the low follow-through to keep the puck close to the ice, waiting for a deflection.

The Snapshot

Amazingly, this shot has only been recognized by hockey coaches as something to teach fairly recently even though it has been around for many decades in a variety of forms. The snapshot was often thought of as a muffed slapshot; a slapshot that a player failed to get away cleanly. This shot, taken from either a standing or skating position, is a sort of one-third slapshot.

With the puck about two feet out in front of him and about three feet off to the side, the player slides and rolls the lower hand on the stick out and down toward the blade while still grasping the shaft. At the same time, with the lower hand, the player is drawing the stick back up off the ice toward a position behind him until the blade is flat to the ice about two to three feet above the ice surface. When the stick has reached this point, it is brought down sharply toward the puck in a sweeping downward arc. As the blade hits the puck, additional reserve energy is transferred to the puck rapidly by the player as the forward momentum meets the puck on the ice, sending it on its way.

There is very little follow-through, maybe only to one or two feet off the ice surface while the lower wrist is then rolled downward. The puck should not be on the ice surface, but about two to three inches above the ice. This is significant because two to three inches above the surface is the perfect height to increase potential deflections of the puck toward the net by either teammates or defenders.

Even without deflections, if the puck is launched correctly to begin with, there is still a good chance it will arrive on net at a very difficult height to defend against—just over the goalie's blade.

The Slapshot

This is the most dramatic of all the shots. It travels the fastest, hits the hardest, and makes the loudest crunch as it smashes against the boards and glass. It is also the hardest shot to learn and master and the easiest shot to look foolish attempting. It is actually a very dangerous shot in many aspects. The height to which the stick is drawn back is often just above shoulder height to face height. It travels the fastest (in the pros, sometimes over a hundred miles an hour) so it is the hardest shot to dodge. Because so much energy and momentum are transferred to the puck, it hits the hardest—in the pros it has often broken goalie's or other player's bones even when they are wearing full pads. Finally, because it is a very tricky, difficult shot to execute—partially because timing is everything — a player who misses the puck can fall unexpectedly and hurt himself (not to mention his confidence and pride).

Incidentally, I do not advocate using the slapshot in mite, squirt, or pee-wee play. The younger players are too vulnerable and impressionable and this could ruin a good hockey career before it even gets started. But for the older players, the slapshot is a very effective weapon against opponents. It is hard and fast and therefore very difficult for anyone to stop. It is intimidating; even if the player shoots off the mark, the next time it's coming in on goal, the goalie may flinch just enough to let it in. It is powerful; it can often find its way through a maze of players and legs into the goal even after multiple deflections. It keeps going through sheer momentum.

The slapshot is executed similarly to the snapshot. The major difference is the height to which the stick is lifted behind the player. For the slapshot, the stick can be lifted up to shoulder height or beyond. Many players will try to lift the stick to a vertical position at this point, but this really doesn't do any good. In fact, it can hinder the shot by telegraphing the move to the defenders. In addition, lifting the stick to vertical makes it take too long to get off the shot this way and requires excess energy. As the stick is brought back down, it should be brought down with both hands. Both hands should be transferring energy to the stick with the upper hand pulling the stick down with the elbow pointing down and the lower hand guiding, pulling down, and then pushing the stick along into

The slapshot is an intimidating offensive weapon. Here the player has great form with weight properly shifted and hands wide apart for maximum transfer of power to the puck.

the puck for the energy transference.

The follow-through is high as well, up to three or four feet, with the blade facing flat to the ice surface, finishing by pointing toward the target. Have your players practice until they are able to keep the puck within three feet of the ice surface. Remember, the goal cage is only four feet high and the puck may deflect up.

Drills

There is no trick to practice shooting, no special gimmick drill. The only way for your players to learn and improve is to gather an ample supply of pucks and shoot, shoot, shoot. But remind them to practice with a purpose. Just shooting aimlessly against a wall doesn't do them any good. Shooting at a specific spot will improve both their aim and their concentration. In the event that a goaltender is not available to shoot against, have your players use a bought or made puck stopper in front of the net. (See Illustration 2-1.)

Basically a puck stopper is a thick board or heavy fabric that totally covers the mouth of the goal and snaps onto the outside goal pipes both vertically and horizontally. Into the cover are holes of various sizes in various locations. The most common locations

ILLUSTRATION 2-1. *A puck stopper is no more than an outline of a goalie on a piece of plywood with holes cut out to practice shooting pucks through usually vulnerable spots.*

are in each corner of the goal representing the areas that a goal-tender does not cover when he is in a crouch. There are also holes right in the middle about eight inches below center representing what is called the five hole or the open space between the goalie's pads when he is down in a crouch. Finally, there is a hole on the left side halfway down. This represents the space left between the goalie's bent arm and his body as he holds the stick. These are the most common shooting and scoring areas that every player should be able to capitalize on from all parts of the ice, for these areas are where a majority of goals are scored.

The shooter should practice his shots from all sections of the ice: from up close and far away; from the face-off circles; from the blue lines; and from in front of the net. The player should practice from the left *and* right wings even if it is the "off wing" (left wing practicing shots from the right wing's position and vice versa). The shooter should practice these different shots while skating quickly, then slowly, then while stationary. Basically, every combination of shot, ice location, and skating speed should be practiced to make the practice sessions worthwhile.

3.

EQUIPMENT

The equipment that hockey players wear today has undergone such a tremendous advance in technology in the past few years that today's player is a modern, sleek, well-defined machine ready to do battle. The weight of the protective equipment has been reduced significantly while the quality of protection has been increased enormously. Flexibility, sometimes nearly nonexistent in some early hockey equipment, is now the standard. Finally, with the introduction of synthetic materials and machine-generated manufacturing, the price of decent, well-fitted equipment is now within the reach of nearly every player on the ice. A good coach will not let his players on the playing surface to do battle with anything less than the required equipment, properly fitted and in good condition.

PROPER EQUIPMENT
Where to Purchase

It is much easier to purchase proper equipment for the player today than it was just a few short years ago. There are large chains of sporting goods stores all over the country that carry a "pro" line of hockey equipment in all price ranges for all ages and skills, but you must know what to buy. These stores might be your first and possibly only consideration when searching for playing gear. There are, however, many other places to purchase equipment.

MAIL ORDER

Once the proper accoutrements for the game of hockey were available only in the pro shops of the rinks or through black and white catalogs of stores in some far-off provinces of Canada. Today, you can still get the required items from mail order houses both in the U.S.

and Canada, and they usually offer the best prices around. Unfortunately, there are some major drawbacks to shopping by mail. Shipping and handling charges often elevate the prices of the inexpensive equipment over local prices. If the equipment is returned, you still may be responsible for paying shipping and handling charges.

In addition, your players cannot try on the equipment for fit until it is in hand some time after the order is placed. If your player knows his size and has worn that specific brand and piece of equipment before, then this works, but if it is a first-time purchase, the player may not know what he is buying. Also, as mentioned previously, there is the time element involved. When ordering through a catalog, your players may have to wait some time to get the pieces ordered. If it's in the middle of the summer and there are no games scheduled, that may be acceptable. But if it is the middle of the hockey season, the players will be sitting on the bench an eternity waiting for the shipment to arrive.

Finally, if you are ordering from a dealer in Canada, there may be customs and import fees. These fees vary. Not all equipment is subject to duty, and not all companies or stores pay it. One famous store in Niagara Falls, Canada has another store in Niagara Falls, New York to fulfill orders from the U.S. to circumvent the fees. Make sure you check the amount of the duty, when and how it must be paid, and who is responsible for it.

PRO SHOPS

Local pro shops are your fastest and easiest bet. They are located in the rink where you practice, are open convenient hours for hockey players, and know how to properly fit a player. In addition, they may offer discounts to their in-house teams and may even have loaner equipment that allows your players to try out some of the supplies before they purchase them. The largest drawback of course is the price. The shops are there to make money and charge the highest possible prices. It helps to look for "end of the season" clearance sales or for last year's models. This equipment is often reduced for quick sale because retailers don't want to store the big boxes over the summer and they want to make room for next year's line. There is nothing wrong with last year's equipment. It is just as good as the next year's models, only maybe not in the hottest color scheme. But who cares what the gear looks like, as long as it does the job of providing protection.

USED EQUIPMENT

Another viable source of equipment is the used equipment trading shop. These establishments are not as prevalent in the U.S. as they should be, and it may take some searching to find them. Some times, larger new equipment retail stores will maintain one of these shops in a back room of the store, certainly out of the way but still very accessible. You can go in and take your time sorting through the equipment, all of which has an asking price that is usually significantly lower than the same equipment new. Sometimes, you can add your own old equipment to sell and get store credit to use toward purchasing new supplies. The retailer either acts as a middle man and takes a cut of the asking price established by the owner of the equipment (consignment sale) or he will act as an equipment reseller by purchasing the equipment outright and selling it for a discount price he determines is fair. In either case, the prices are reasonable and the equipment is good. If there is not a store like this in your area, why not consider starting one? It doesn't even have to be year round. Maybe you can open up shop in a garage for just the first few months of the season until everybody gets their supplies. The kids get a kick out of helping out, parents (or maybe a team looking for a fund raiser) find a small business to bring in a little extra income, and everyone is happy to be buying quality equipment at a discount.

Finally, don't forget to check the "For Sale" signs or bulletin board at the rinks you visit. There is always someone selling something. You may find just what you are looking for. Again, if there is not a board like this at your rink, why not start one? Ask the rink owner if you can put up a board, ask where to put it, and let him know that you will get someone to be the board monitor who is responsible for all of the postings on it so it doesn't look like a junk pile. I think the owners will appreciate your concern and give you the go-ahead. If they don't, you can always start an equipment swap newsletter and pass it out at games to all the parents and kids there. It can't hurt. Of course, as the owner (proprietor, editor, manager, supervisor) of any venture, you will get first "dibs" on whatever gear comes in for best selection and price. You see, there's a method to my madness for your benefit.

It should be remembered that as I added suggestions from retail store down to swap newsletter, the level of support, advice, and guidance in selecting equipment diminished to nothing. As a courtesy, you may want to have someone knowledgeable about equipment, like a coach or trainer, available as a non-binding "consultant" to answer questions parents or players may have concerning the equipment that you are not comfortable answering yourself.

IMPROPER EQUIPMENT

Please do not allow any child to play ice hockey with street hockey equipment. Whether it is your child or someone else's, it is dangerous! As a coach, I will not let the child play and neither should you. Street hockey gear is just not made to accept the punishment or, more importantly, offer the protection of ice hockey equipment. The street hockey equipment may be expensive, look nice, and already be part of the player's equipment bag, but it is not safe to use on the ice. It is often made of "mystery material" surrounding reinforced cardboard and plastic. The cardboard gets wet and crumbles or the plastic gets cold and brittle and shatters. The "leather" is just cheap synthetic material that cracks and offers no support. Don't even bother to send your child to the rink with this equipment and if you are coaching others, do not let them on the ice with it — not with street hockey gloves, sticks, helmets, masks, shin guards, elbow pads, or shoulder pads, nothing! As a coach, I will *not* let the player on the ice for his or her own personal safety—and your child's coach shouldn't either.

PROPER FIT

In most cases, common sense will tell you when equipment is fitted properly. All of the equipment, especially the helmet and face guard, must fit snugly against the body without binding (binding restricts blood flow) and also without permitting large gaping spaces. Straps should be adjusted so they are snug but not tight. None of the pads should be flapping around under the jersey. The reason a player needs the equipment to fit close to the body is simply that you do not want to provide any open unprotected spaces that a puck might creep into when on the fly.

If you are unsure what size to purchase for your player, don't worry too much. You can always turn to your hockey professional for advice. Also, each manufacturer either prints a chart of correct sizing and measuring of equipment (taking into account a player's size, weight, age, and experience) or clearly marks on the attached tags the equipment size and the size player it should fit. Take the time to read this information or write to the manufacturer for more information. Manufacturers are more than happy to do what they can to get you to buy their products for your player(s).

Helmet

A secure-fitting helmet is far and above the most important piece of safety equipment a player owns. It must fit exactly as intended by the manufacturer. The helmet and face shield provide optimum protection to the most vital and fragile part of the body. Players can recover from broken arms or fingers, but may never recover from brain injury. Make sure that the head is protected as best as you can protect it. Spare no expense in getting the best

Here is a well-protected player with proper headgear: wire cage mask with safety clips and protective ear flaps.

equipment available to safeguard the skull and face.

Obviously, vision on the playing surface is a priority. A secure helmet will keep the field of vision open to the skater because it cannot twist and turn or fall backward or forward on his head. If possible, get help from the hockey professional at the pro shop to get a proper fit and read the instructions carefully and completely before fitting the helmet.

Pads

If the pads are too big, besides the fact that they may weigh too much for the particular player, they may become entangled with other equipment either on the wearer or on other players as they get into corner skirmishes. In addition, pads that are too large cannot provide as adequate protection over the sensitive areas as the manufacturers designed them to provide. If the pads are too large and droop too far down, sensitive and painful areas of the body such as shoulders, collarbones, knees, or groin are left unprotected as the padding ends up protecting the area three to four inches below the intended section.

GETTING DRESSED

Do not let youngsters get into bad habits while dressing themselves in the locker room. Little players (and even some of the bigger ones) are often so anxious to get out onto the ice that they haphazardly throw on the equipment without regard to proper fit or order of dress. Teach them from the very beginning the proper and correct way to fit and put on their equipment.

The coach should check or at least "eyeball" each player and his equipment as he is getting dressed or as he enters the ice for proper equipment and fit. As a coach of younger players, I once had to hold a session on how to get dressed. Parents buy all of this equipment and give it to the player to use, and the next time they see their child with the gear, she is out on the ice with the equipment covered with a huge floppy jersey. The parents don't really even know if she has any equipment on underneath the jersey, much less if it is the proper equipment properly adjusted. Take a short time to teach your players the correct procedures.

I'm going to assume that on a mixed team of girls and boys, each gender has its own locker room or at least dressing area. If this isn't the case and the two sexes are forced to dress out together, you may want to instruct your team to dress partially at home. If you do make that adjustment, you might share this information with the parents of your players so that they can help their young ones follow the procedures for getting dressed.

Forwards and Defensemen

INNER LAYER

To begin the inner layer, each player should strip down to his or her basic underwear, that is light cotton underpants and undershirt and thin light cotton socks. Light cotton against the skin will help draw off sweat from the body and transmit it to the outer garments. Over the cotton foundation, the player would be best off wearing a one-piece cotton "union suit" (one-piece long johns that cover the body from neck to ankles). Two-piece suits have a tendency to split at the waist after a few shifts, and if the cotton undergarments are two-piece as well, the opening can expose bare flesh to the cold ice surface. Some players prefer to wear a short-sleeved union suit because they feel too cramped in the upper body with long sleeves. That's no problem; the middle area is the area of concern addressed by a one-piece suit.

Finish off the inner layer with a pair of good quality medium-weight athletic sweat socks over the thin cotton socks and up over the union suit legs. The body is now adequately protected from the cold at all points. It also has a built-in absorption system to draw sweat, which can get pretty cold between long shifts, away from the body's skin surface.

Middle Layer

The middle layer must start off with the athletic protector (cup) for males. If possible, try to get one specifically designed for hockey as they are a little bit larger and sturdier. One hockey equipment company now manufactures a style of shorts that pulls up over the union suit and ties with a drawstring at the waist. The player can slip the cup into a built-in pouch which holds it securely to eliminate the cup supporter. These shorts also have a series of Velcro strips around the legs to press the tops of the socks against to hold them up. This eliminates the sock garter. Of course, the importance of a secure and properly fitted cup cannot be overstated. If your male players do not have the above described shorts cup set, they will need to have and wear two additional belts around their waists, one each for the cup and socks. Female players will still need a garter or sock support system to hold up their socks.

After the cup and garters (or shorts) are in place, put the shin guards on the legs and secure them firmly with the straps. Some players prefer not to use the straps but simply use the pressure of the tightness of the socks to hold the guards against the legs. They then secure the pads with tape over the socks. It eliminates the straps cutting into the backs of the legs and allows for better circulation. This method is not recommended for the younger, less-developed players, since they often do not have sufficient leg muscle definition to hold the guards in place. It's like putting leg guards on a pole and shaking the pole all around; they simply will not remain facing outward.

The size selection of shin guards or most any of the equipment is easy. On most of the shipping bags for the guards, the length of the guards and the leg lengths they fit are clearly marked. Measure the leg from the ball of the knee cap to the instep and choose pads that fit that measurement. Proper fit is essential here. As a player will use his shin guards to stop a lot of pucks, you want to make sure that as much of the leg as possible is properly protected. Too long a shin guard will hinder skating ability and ankle flexibility. Too short a guard provides inadequate protection.

After the shin guards are secured in place, they are covered with hockey socks. The socks should be pulled up tight and attached at the tops to either the Velcro or the garter tabs. If the player has stirrup-less socks, warn them not to pull too hard or the socks will come halfway up the leg. Once the socks are secured, the player should stand up and adjust them for a comfortable fit.

The next step is to pull the hockey pants on and up, but not to fasten them yet. While the arms and waist are not restricted, the skates should be put on. The player can get a good feel for tightness and fit before his movement is restricted by the secured pants or by the upper body equipment. Also, the sooner you get all the players in their skates, the lower the chances of anyone losing toes as other players move by open stalls with their skates on.

Once the skates are comfortable, have the player stand up and secure the pants with the laced drawstring. Pants are usually measured according to the player's waist size with an extra four to six inches built in for movement. The pants have all of their padding secured by stitching into the legs, side, and back panels of the pants, so there is usually nothing to adjust but the waist. Some players also wear suspenders on their pants. If a player likes a lot of freedom in his pants, he can lace them more loosely and wear suspenders. If he likes the pants tighter around the waist, he can leave off the suspenders. This option is strictly up to the player—whichever he feels most comfortable with is fine. Players can also use both methods if they prefer, but they cannot leave both off. It would be quite embarrassing to anyone to be skating in on a breakaway and have his pants fall down!

The next step is to put the shoulder pads on over the head (and over the suspenders if they are being worn). The arms go through the loops in the arm flaps that hang down to the sides. The adjustment and fit of the shoulder pads are critical. If you examine the pads closely, you will see that they are really two distinct halves laced together. The player should try on the pads with someone to help adjust the laces for a secure fit in both the front and back. Again, make sure that the pads are secure and snug fitting.

For female players, manufacturers have special shoulder pads with extra long extensions down the front to protect the breasts. These extensions may also have a cupped feature of hard plastic shells for added fit, comfort, and protection. The extensions have an elastic band at the bottom of the pads that go around the back for better fit and security. All girls, regardless of their physical development, should wear these shoulder pads with the extra protection.

Once the pads are properly adjusted, the player need only untie the front laces to put them on or remove them. In this manner, they are easily adjusted by the player in the locker room, with a little extra effort to correct the fit as a game progresses, or as a player grows.

Elbow pads come next. In the past few years, elbow pads have developed and evolved from thin little foam rubber pads to high-tech polyurethane-injected protective devices. Before, they covered and protected only the elbow. Now they cover and protect the parts of the arm left unprotected between the gloves and shoulder pads. If the player is using older, borrowed equipment, he may want to update the equipment in this area. If a player has pads that you are unsure about in terms of protection, go to the pro shop and see how the new pads differ from those on hand. If there is not a significant difference, don't worry. But if there are noticeable differences, then I would encourage an investment in protection.

Some leagues mandate the use of back/spinal protection. The back/spinal pad is a long, thin, flexible pad that goes down the back to cover the spine from the neck to the tailbone. It is secured with arm loops and waist straps. Check local league rules to see if this pad is mandated. Even if it is not, it is a good idea to use one.

Another useful pad to consider is the neck whiplash collar or the horse collar made popular by football players. It protects against neck injuries. Again, check local league rules regarding the mandatory use of this pad, but I think they are useful protectors.

OUTER LAYER

That's it for the middle layer of equipment. Now for the final outer layer. The jersey will probably be provided by the team so there is little choice in this matter other than size. If given options, choose a larger, looser shirt into which the player can grow, but do not choose an enormous one. A jersey that is too small will be too confining and uncomfortable and will not provide the necessary freedom of movement. It is important that the player not feel confined, but if the jersey is too big, equipment and pucks can get tangled up in the folds, especially when the player is in the corner digging for the puck. A jersey that is too large becomes a liability. It is very easy for an opponent to grab and hold onto a really large jersey out of the sight of the referee. Regardless of this advice, there are times when the team jerseys have to be doled out and there is no option but to give someone a shirt that is way too large. If you have a player with a jersey that is dangerously big, ask him to tuck it in. If he is concerned that it may look at little weird, point out that some of the NHL players are making this style quite popular. Who knows, more of the teammates may want to tuck theirs in just to look stylish.

The next piece of equipment to put on is the helmet. We have already discussed the helmet and its fit. All of your players must have a helmet from a list of helmets approved for play in ice hockey by at least one of the two governing bodies of amateur ice hockey. It is easy to check a helmet for this endorsement as the manufacturers apply a sticker to the back of the helmet near the neck line. The sticker is about an inch in diameter and states if the helmet is approved for play and at what level of play. Do not remove this sticker. A good referee or coach will check quickly for these stickers on the helmets of all the players on the ice and will not allow a player to play unless she has an approved ice hockey helmet. This of course is for the player's own protection. These helmets have undergone rigorous punishment and testing to meet specific accepted standards and can withstand the force of a puck shot at high velocity.

Another essential part of the helmet is the face guard. Every non-professional league requires the players to wear face guards. The face guard is usually a wire cage mask that attaches to the front of the helmet near the top of the forehead band and covers the entire face down to below the chin. It is secured with either a separate strap or a replacement strap that secures both the helmet and the face guard to the head. Just any old face guard won't do— the face guard, like the helmet, must be approved for play. Guards that have large openings around the eyes, that do not have sufficiently strong wire, that have sharp edges protruding beyond the edges, or that do not cover the entire face are generally not acceptable. Most manufacturers attach a small tag to the face guard stating if it is approved for play or not. This tag can be removed. Some leagues may require only one specific brand or type. Check with league officials as to which types are acceptable.

Another type of face guard that has been recently approved for tournament play is the plastic face shield. This clear plastic guard resembles a motorcycle face guard and covers and protects the face like a cage. The shield has a series of air openings across the bottom of the guard for ventilation. It is attached and secures just like the wire cage guards. It is available in full face models and half-face eye guards. Only the full face models are approved for play in the amateur ranks.

There are advantages and disadvantages to the full plastic face guard. On the positive side, players claim they feel better protected, they can see more of the ice, and they are not distracted by the metal bars that run horizontally and vertically across the field of vision in the wire cage mask. On the negative side, the shield can often fog up; it scratches easily and is expensive; and, in contrast to the above feedback, some players say they feel *less* protected with a plastic shield. You can get anti-fog wipe for the shield to help with fog-ups. You can buy protective bags for the helmet to guard against scratches. You can find the shield on sale for a reasonable price if you look. As for protection, companies have tested the shields and they can withstand the force of a flying puck without shattering.

As a coach, I personally have no preference for my players. I let them choose as long as their guard is approved for play. As a goalie, I prefer the wire cage. I do feel better protected, but I like the feel of the cold breeze from the ice surface against my face to cool me down. This sensation doesn't occur with the plastic guards. But that's just personal preference.

As a coach, and as a speech-language pathologist and hearing professional, I also prefer to have the players wear helmets with full ear guards. I know and appreciate the sensitivity of the ears and hearing, and I know the value of hearing in life. One good whack with a puck or stick against the ear can send your hearing out the door permanently. Without hearing, it is very difficult, if not impossible, to play hockey. I admit I don't get much cooperation from my players on this point. They claim they can't hear their teammates with their ears covered and prefer to leave the flaps off. I wear full ear flaps on my helmet and I don't have difficulty hearing through them. I have been lobbying the league to make these flaps mandatory but so far with no luck. The only way players will wear ear flaps is if they are smart, or if their league and/or parents mandate them. Whether you are a coach or a parent, or both, lobby your league to require ear flaps.

There is *yet* another piece of equipment that needs to be worn on the face. Every player on the ice in amateur hockey *must* wear a mouth guard, and must have the guard *in place* in order to play. It only needs to be that small piece of moldable rubber that fits in the mouth, but it should be worn. It goes a long way toward protecting the teeth and protecting a player from biting through his lips and tongue when hit by either a puck or a check. Many leagues value this small device so highly that the referees are instructed to stop a game immediately when they see a mouth guard is either spit out or knocked out. I have also seen a league where the referees disallowed a goal because the scorer was not wearing a mouth guard at the time. They take this protection very seriously and so should you. Interestingly, it is one piece of equipment about which the players do not complain. They take it as a matter of course. Start the very youngest players out wearing one from the beginning and they'll get used to it quickly.

We've already discussed the stick in a previous chapter so there is no need to do so here. But what holds the stick is important. The hockey glove is probably the most distinctive looking piece of equipment that a player wears. It has strange padding and rolls on the back of the hands, and long massive fingers that are intimidating to the casual observer. But the glove really is a work of art. With ultra high-tech styling, it is designed to give ultimate protection to the back of the hand, yet be flexible on the palm side to be able to "baby" a puck into a minuscule opening. Most gloves are essentially the same except for size. As players' hands come in all sizes, so do gloves. Keep trying on different brands and styles and sizes until you come across one that feels comfortable to you. Players should wear these gloves around the house to break them in, and practice holding the sticks with them as much as possible.

The one significant design variation of the glove is the length of the cuff, or the collar that extends up the arm from the wrist. Forwards and pure shooters prefer a short cuff—about an inch to two inches long—to give them significant flexibility in wrist movement to fire the puck. Defensemen prefer a longer cuff—four to six inches long—to afford maximum protection while blocking shots. Although this cuff styling seems to be the trend, it is by no means the standard. The player should use whichever style feels most comfortable, but make sure the cuff allows him to play efficiently.

Well, that's about it for the forwards and defensemen as they get dressed. Putting on all this equipment correctly should only take ten to fifteen minutes so it's not as overwhelming as it looks. Every piece of gear is essential for safe play. When worn correctly, the player is as well suited to do battle as the knights of old, and better protected against injury. The total cost of all the equipment, considering about middle price range for each piece, is between $150.00 to $200.00 not including skates. But if you think that's a lot of equipment, let's take a look at what a goaltender wears.

Goaltenders

Goaltenders need tremendous freedom of movement. The position of goalie requires at least much as flexibility as that required of any other athlete in any other sport in the world. Hockey goalies must have all of this flexibility while wearing more equipment in weight and volume than any other player on (or off) the ice.

INNER LAYER

The foundation for the goaltender as he or she dresses is exactly the same as that of a forward or defenseman. First the thin cotton undergarments, then long johns over them. Leave any particular adjustments concerning sleeve length or suit weight to the individual players after they have played in a few matches. They will be better able to tell you what works for them and what doesn't. Then you can help them adjust accordingly.

MIDDLE LAYER

To begin the middle layer, male goaltenders wear a very special, highly protective cup. Unlike a cup in a pouch, it is a one-piece unit that is much thicker and heavier than a normal protective device. Both the cup and the edge roll bands are wider, and it has a wider, more protective waistband. It is designed to protect the entire groin

The two different types of skates worn while playing hockey. Note the added protection of the goalie skate on the right.

area from all angles, not just head on. The goalie may never know where the next shot is coming from and must be ready at all times to take the force of the puck. Obviously, with someone shooting the puck right at him and it being his job to get in its way, a goalie needs all the protection he can get.

Next come special knee guards. The guards are secured by two wide elastic and Velcro straps around the back of the leg. They are easily adjusted for fit as they are put on. They have an upper extension that protects the thigh rising about six to eight inches above the knee. A goalie needs this area protected when he drops down onto his knees to stop a shot. The bottom of the pant leg tends to creep up in this situation and expose an area between the top of the leg pad and the bottom of the pant leg. A lot of rebound shots come in hard and quick and at a height to hit this spot—three to five inches off the ice.

After the knee pads, the goalie may strap on protective calf muscle pads to the side of the legs, but these individual pads are becoming more rare as most new exterior leg pads have incorporated calf protectors as a standard feature. After these pieces are in place, the team socks are put on and secured with a garter.

Next come the special goalie pants. They are unique because they are protected with extra thick padding in all areas around the leg, especially in the front, where a goalie takes on direct shots, and in between the legs, where the very sensitive inner thigh is exposed when the goalie does the "splits." In addition, the pants are usually much larger in size to accommodate this extra padding and to make the goaltender "bigger"; that is, they give the goaltender more area with which to stop and trap the puck. Remember to have the goalie put on his skates next before he ties his pants.

Goalie skates are also highly specialized equipment. You already know about the thick and straight blade. In addition, the boot of the skate is made of special reinforced padded leather which is then surrounded by a high impact polyurethane shell. This allows the goalie to take shots directly to the foot without worrying about breaking bones. The blade support has special extended plastic tabs jutting up between the main supports to prevent pucks from squirming in between them. Finally, the skate boots are shorter up the leg and do not have the Achilles tendon protector on the back. This small adjustment allows the goalie to bend the foot more easily to get down to the ice more quickly. Make sure that the goalies tie their skates as they want them to feel in the game—they won't have the opportunity to adjust the laces once they put their leg pads on.

The most distinctive feature of the goalie, and the heaviest and most expensive pads a goalie wears, are the leg pads. Put them on next. There is a left and a right pad so make sure they have them sorted correctly. The attaching straps will buckle to the inside and the thick vertical rolls will be on the outside. Also make sure they are pushed down low onto the skate toe tops. There is an additional strap at the bottom of each pad to attach it to the skate through the supports at the toe. Start at the toe and work your way up the leg buckling and adjusting as necessary for fit. Lastly attach the upper calf straps securely. You do not want the pad tops flapping down onto the ice as you go down to stop a shot. Like a lot of goalie equipment, these pads have undergone radical changes in the past few years. They used to be constructed of leather shells hand stuffed with deer hair, now they are made of synthetic materials stuffed with more synthetic material. The major advantages of the new pads are the reduction in weight (they are extremely lightweight now); durability (they never seem to wear out); water resistance (they do not absorb sweat or water); and protection (the synthetic material is a better shock absorber). The major disadvantage is price as they are more expensive than ever. One consolation is that when a player reaches physical maturity, the pads will probably last the rest of his hockey life. Another comfort is knowing that when the player does outgrow the pads, they have a terrific resale value.

Once these pads are in place, the goalie can stand up and secure his pants. Most goalies prefer to use only suspenders to keep the pants from falling down as some feel the drawstring around the waist inhibits free turning. Many goalies also feel like a sack of potatoes if they tie the pants tightly because the pants are so much larger than normal.

Believe it or not, we are almost finished. The next item on the goalie's wardrobe agenda is the body protector. This is another area in which great advances have been made for both protection and comfort. The goaltender now pulls a one-piece protection "system" over his head instead of the two or three separate pieces previously required. The "system" consists of full-length (down to the wrists) shoulder and arm protectors attached to a full-length (below the waist) body chest protector and also a half- to full-length back protector. This system takes the place of the old three-piece system which consisted of arm pads, shoulder pads, and chest protector. Now all these components are laced together into one piece that the goalie can pull over the head like a heavy shirt.

Just as with the other equipment, the adjustments for fit should be made at home well in advance of the game. A parent or friend should do the adjusting while the goalie, in a crouch, relays how the adjustments feel. Once the piece is adjusted, there is nothing else to lace or adjust. It goes on and slips off as one complete system over the head with arms going through the arm protectors. Even this piece of equipment has a left and right side. Goaltenders who catch with the left hand will have a special flat surface attached to the "system" facing out toward the shooter halfway up the inside of the left arm for additional protection. The stick arms also have additional padding on the outside of the arm protector halfway up above the blocker glove top to help stop shots and provide protection.

Depending on local league rules, the goaltender may be required to wear neck protection. There are three types of neck guards that are generally in use. There is the reinforced foam rubber turtleneck type collar that completely encircles the neck. This type is not popular with most goalies due to tight restraints and supposed difficulty in turning the head from side to side and in looking down. If a goalie wears this type, it fastens with Velcro around the neck before putting on the body protector.

The next type of collar is the bib collar. This style consists of a short padded plastic "priest" collar with a larger plastic bib down the front. This collar helps protect against damage to the collarbones. It is secured by Velcro straps in the back and is quite comfortable. This is my personal choice. It is worn over the body protector but under the jersey. The third and most popular type of neck protection is the curved clear plastic shield that dangles down from the helmet in front of the neck area. It is attached by laces to the chin straps of the helmet and is free swinging. Goaltenders do not actually wear them, their helmet wears them and they go on with the helmet and cage.

Check into the local rules to see what special equipment is required (such as neck guards). Even if the neck guard is not mandated, I highly recommend it. A few years ago in the NHL, a goalie was slashed across the throat by an errant skate blade in a tangle up in front of the net. He lost considerable blood and almost lost his life. It took a long time for him to return to full playing status, and even then, his confidence must have been shaken. He was not wearing a neck protector at the time of the accident. With a neck protector, chances are it would not have happened; at the very least it would not have been as severe.

OUTER LAYER

That's it for what you don't see under the jersey. Now for what you do see. Although many local teams will be either unable or unwilling to spend the extra for the special jersey, there is a special jersey for the goaltender. A goalie's jersey has a special "goalie cut": fuller cut around the chest and upper arm areas, tapering down to normal around the waist and to less than normal around the wrists. It obviously allows for the jersey to fit comfortably around the waist, lower arms, and neck without being too baggy, while it allows room elsewhere for the goalie's extra equipment. Pucks and equipment don't become entangled in the shirt, yet the tapered sleeves fit nicely into the gloves without bulk. Your goalie will appreciate the special jersey, but it is expensive and usually not part of the budget.

After the jersey, the helmet goes on. It should be exactly like the helmet worn by the forwards and defensemen (except for the possibility of the added neck protector). The cage is the same and the player should even use the same type of mouth protector. The helmet should be adjusted the same and worn the same.

Once the helmet is adjusted and the face guard secured, the gloves are next. On one hand goes the catching mitt. It resembles a highly modified first baseman's mitt with a lot of extra protection on both the front catching surface and on the back knuckle surface where skates can cut across the back of the hand. In addition, it has a heavily protected cuff extending up the wrist for six or seven inches. This cuff over the wrist is what faces the shooter ready for the catch. It also has a "cheater" bar that extends from the tip of the thumb to the top of the cuff, sometimes nine or ten inches. This "cheater" is metal-covered leather that gives the glove a larger stopping area. Finally, the webbing of the glove is extended several inches beyond the glove profile. It is reinforced to take punish-ment and is slightly hooked over at the top to prevent the puck from slipping through. Sizing of this glove is very important. Too big a glove is too heavy and sloppy on the hand, and a goalie needs a lightning quick hand to catch the puck. Get just as much glove as a player can hold up steadily for an extended period of time. If the player begins to droop that arm down after only a few minutes, the glove is too big or too heavy. Shooters will take advantage of this fact every opportunity they get and shoot high to the glove side. They know the goalie will never get the puck.

The blocker mitt, or stick mitt, goes on the other hand, the hand that holds the stick. This mitt was originally called the "waf-fle" because of its resemblance to an old waffle iron—square with holes in it. The blocker is simply a rectangular piece of plastic and impact foam covered with leather and attached to the back of a protective leather glove. The mitt no longer has the holes that were once cut to expose the plastic below. These holes were supposedly there to help the goalie direct incoming shots away from the net into the corners. It was found that this could be done just as well without the holes.

The inside glove is made of thick leather and a highly pro-tected thumb to prevent damage when the goalie turns the stick and hand out to block a shot, exposing the thumb. This thumb has a leather strap attaching it to the main blocker to prevent it from being bent backward. The blocker should come no higher than three inches below the elbow bend and no lower than an inch below the extended fingertips in the glove. Make sure that your goalie does not buy a blocker that is too large or too heavy, as he is already holding a heavy stick. As with the catching mitt, if there is too much weight for the goalie to comfortably hold his hands high, he will be unable to block shots headed for the upper corners. Again, shooters who notice this fact will take advantage of it and shoot for those corners.

Lastly, the goalie needs a stick. The goalie's stick is special too. The blade or paddle of the stick is up to 3½ inches wide. This width continues along the full 15½ inch blade and turns up the shaft at the bend for about 24 inches at which point it meets the thin shaft. Like other sticks, a goalie stick can be too long or too short. It is measured to the chin just as described in the section on sticks in Chapter Two. Reread this section if you need a refresher course regarding the importance of a properly chosen stick. Improp-er length can adversely affect the player.

The goalie holds the stick with the blocker mitt glove at the joint between the thin shaft and the paddle. There is a new design

The goalie is ready for anything. His equipment is used for blocking shots as well as covering and protecting every inch of his body.

in goalie sticks where the thin shaft is bent slightly for a few inches giving the stick a sort of warped look. This is not a manufacturing flaw, it is a design innovation. It is difficult for a goaltender wearing a heavy blocker mitt to pick up a straight stick lying flat on the ice surface. With the curved shaft, the stick has a sort of built-in handle by which to be lifted. It really works!

Well, there you have it. All the necessary equipment for an individual to play goaltender. It should take a goalie twenty-five to thirty minutes to get dressed properly. Once fully dressed out, they are the most protected athletes on the planet. Unfortunately, goalies are also among the most expensive athletes to dress. Taking an average price for the equipment discussed above, the total cost will be between $600.00 and $700.00. For that price, they better be well protected!

Equipment Bag

Each player should have a hockey equipment bag to carry all his gear. These bags are a necessity. Some teams may provide team bags for their players' use. If you are the coach, consider this option. If you are a parent, it is your job as a parent to make sure that your player has a functional bag. The equipment bag should be quite large, water-repellent, and have ventilation holes. A good hockey bag will only cost ten to twenty dollars and do the job very well. Due to the bulk of the goalie's extra equipment, the goalie bag is larger and a bit more expensive.

TEAM EQUIPMENT AND SUPPLIES

Each team should establish and maintain its own hockey supply chest. This chest should remain with the team at all times, both at home and on the road. Whatever physical "chest" your team decides on is quite acceptable, but I have always found that a medium footlocker with handles works best. These are light, cheap, easy to carry, and have all the necessary features such as a locking system and removable tray. Our team manager is responsible for our supply chest's upkeep and restocking and also its transportation to and from the games.

We divide the chest into two parts; a basic first aid kit and a larger equipment area. On the top tray of the chest, we keep necessary basic medical supplies. This first aid kit consists of the following:

First Aid Kit

- ❏ adhesive bandages
- ❏ disinfectant soap
- ❏ elastic bandage wrap
- ❏ heat bags
- ❏ ice bags
- ❏ medical tape
- ❏ any other medical device that individual players may require such as inhalers or special creams
- ❏ a complete medical history card for each player (required by our league) in the event of any serious medical emergency

We are prepared to handle most minor medical emergencies such as scrapes, small cuts, abrasions, and bruises. It should be understood that "the box" is a minor repair facility. It is nothing more than a large first aid box, and anything above the small cut, bruise, scrape, or minor strain must be handled by medical professionals. We are *not* and do not claim to be doctors or emergency technicians. Anything beyond these minor repairs is left to the emergency room at the hospital.

After any treatment from the medical box, we follow up with a call to the parents to inform them of the situation. If there is a serious injury or medical emergency, the rink will call an ambulance and one of the team managers will accompany the player to the hospital with the medical history card listed above.

Game Supplies

In the deeper bottom of the box is the heart and soul of the team. Without this box, we literally couldn't play. In the bottom we carry the following items:

❏ a supply of practice pucks (about two dozen)—used to warm up at the beginning of the games or in practice

❏ two or three perfect condition game pucks—each home team is required to provide these

❏ two spare blank jerseys—just in case anyone forgets his or one is damaged during a game

❏ a few rolls of colored tape in team colors—for putting a number on a spare jersey or taping the lineups to the wall

❏ a half dozen water bottles

❏ a half dozen white towels

❏ blank play sheets—to diagram impromptu plays

❏ skate sharpening stones

❏ a "lock box" — for holding the players' valuables including money, jewelry, and keys

❏ needle and thread (all colors and weights)—for miscellaneous needs

❏ miscellaneous supplies—such as skate laces, equipment laces, chin straps, new mouthpieces, buckles, suspenders, or anything that might break in the locker room or on the ice.

With our team box, (decorated with our team logo and colors, of course) we are prepared to handle almost any emergency or inconvenience that arises.

Well, there you have it. Your entire team is now outfitted to play the game. Every player has all the equipment he needs and it is on and secured properly. The team manager is prepared for the best and the worst that might happen. The ice is waiting. But as you, the coach, get out onto the ice, where do you put all these kids and what do they do when they get there? In the next chapter you'll learn all about positions and position play.

4.

POSITION PLAY

There are six distinct playing positions in ice hockey. They are right and left wing, right and left defense, center, and goaltender. Most often, for the sake of clarity, they are grouped into the three categories of forwards, defensemen, and goaltender. Although this position naming refers to the general areas of responsibility on the ice covered by an individual in the course of a game, the terms by no means do justice to the highly specialized skills required of each player at each specific ice location.

A center employs significantly different skills than a wing in performance of his specific duty, and a left defenseman will not, and often cannot, do the same things as the right defenseman or else there is potential that a hole to the goalie will open wide.

The differences between positions are quite distinguishable and recognized, and the responsibilities associated with each position will be addressed in this section. No position is, however, totally isolated from the rest of the positions in the game. There is a great deal of overlap between the grouped positions and that is why most players are just as comfortable playing the right wing as they are playing center. It is extremely rare, however, for a player to formally move from offense to defense except in emergencies as the skills have little carryover.

A player may be called on to move from defense to offense for it can be assumed that everybody knows how to score goals. Obviously, that is not necessarily true. Even if it were, scoring goals is not the only requirement of an offensive player. You will not see a player shifted between offensive and defensive positions in a game with any regularity. A forward always has a difficult time making the transition to defense ("D"), while defensemen are usually not comfortable playing offense ("O"). Although players will accept added responsibilities, they prefer not to. In youth hockey, I believe that a player needs to learn his own position completely before he gets confused by playing other positions. As a player matures, you may attempt position shifts, but until that time, encourage players to stick with one position. As the coach, the best encouragement you can give is to be consistent with the players. This helps them become confident in their ability to fill their positions.

For the sake of clarity, I will group the players into the known groups of forwards, defensemen, and goaltenders. When there are specific differences in skills that need to be discussed (the ability of a center to take a face-off, for example), I will address them as necessary. But overall, I will refer to the necessary general skills and abilities and the substantive differences between positions that a player needs to acquire to improve himself at his chosen task. The specific ice positions and covered ice areas are as follows. Imagine looking down onto the ice surface from high above center ice.

ZONES

From above, divide the ice lengthwise equally into three separate zones running the full length of the ice from one end board to the other. These are roughly considered the offensive and defensive lanes of a player's position divided equally by the vertical red and blue lines. If your team is attacking the goal to the right, for example, the zone in the center of the ice is the domain of the center. The zone at the bottom of the rink is the right wing zone and the zone at the top is for the left wing. The wings are reversed for the opposing team so the right wing is at the top facing the attacking left wing and the left wing is facing the attacking right wing. The center positions remain opposing each other. As you can see in Illustration 4-1, there is also some curving of the wing zones behind the net both offensively and defensively. These zones will also be considered.

If you are a player and are unsure which position to attempt or if you're a coach and have no idea where to place a particular child, this guide may help you choose. By examining the talents necessary or preferred for each position, a parent, coach, or player may find it easier to decide which position the player is better suited for given his current talents. It may also help a player who is looking to change positions know what skill areas to work on in his game to make a successful transition from one position to the other.

FORWARDS

Forwards can be divided into two styles of players: offensive forwards and defensive forwards. The most recognizable and easily

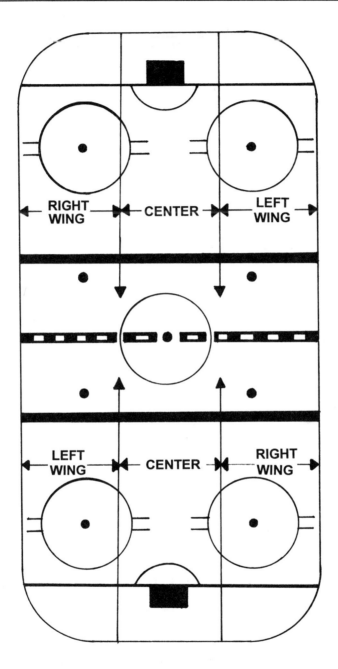

ILLUSTRATION 4-1. *The offensive lanes for the forward lines. Notice how the right and left wings are facing each other on the attack.*

understood style is the scoring forward.

The *primary* responsibility of the forward in hockey was and still is to score. The player scores by putting the puck into the net or by helping another player score by passing the puck to that open player (assisting). In order for the team to present a balanced offensive attack with each offensive player playing at his optimum, each individual must know and fulfill the role and responsibilities associated with the position to which he is assigned.

Defensive Forwards

The forward's responsibilities do not stop with scoring goals. It would be nice if he were able to concentrate on doing just that, for scoring goals wins games. But the goals only stand for a win if the other team does not score a higher number of goals. Over the years, coaches have given this dilemma careful consideration. As a result, the defensive specialist was born. There are, in fact, many defensive specialists who are forwards, and they are known throughout the league as defensive forwards. It is now such a respected position that the Frank J. Selke Trophy is awarded annually to recognize the skill in the NHL. This trophy is awarded "to the forward who best excels in the defensive aspects of the game" as selected in a poll by the Professional Hockey Writers' Association. Even in youth hockey, defensive forward is a position that should be considered for many of the players. They will not all be natural scorers like Wayne Gretzky, Mario Lemieux, or Eric Lindros. Some could be defensive specialists like Dirk Graham, Esa Tikkanen, or Steve Larmer. These highly respected defensive forwards would be welcome additions to any team.

Even the most talented scoring forwards are expected to play some defense during their shift. If nothing else, they should at least fore-check and back-check. Fore-checking is when the attacking team, in the attack zone, checks the opposing defensive players to help set up a scoring opportunity. Back-checking is when the defending team, in its own defensive zone, checks the opposing offensive players as they attack in order to gain or maintain control of the puck to help stop scoring chances and clear the zone of the puck. Neutral zone checking is when both teams are hitting each other in the neutral zone between the two blue lines in order to gain control of the puck when control has not been established. This neutral zone checking is a strict requirement of forwards, more so than the other types of checking they must do, for it is neutral zone checking that helps initiate the offensive plays that lead to scoring chances.

When in the attack zone, the wings will be checking close to

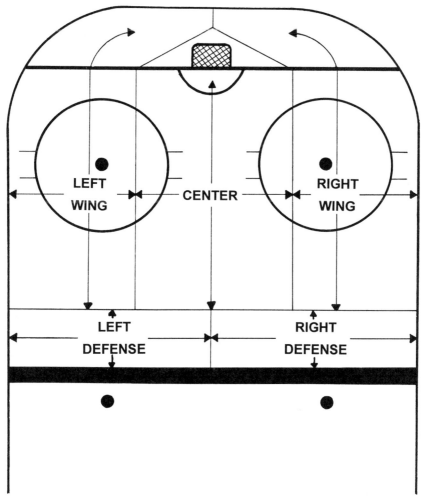

ILLUSTRATION 4-2. *Normal attack zone coverage by an offensive team.*

the boards out to a little beyond the face-off dots and also curving behind the net. The center will be cruising the slot area between the four face-off dots and in toward the goal, checking all defensive players as they touch the puck. The areas out toward the blue lines, known as the points, are left for the defensemen to cover.

The defensemen, however, cannot cover these areas at all times. On occasion, the defenseman on one side will be pulled in off the blue line to close a hole left open by an offensive player— usually a wing—as he is either pulled out of position by a defender or is knocked to the ice and cannot cover his assigned territory.

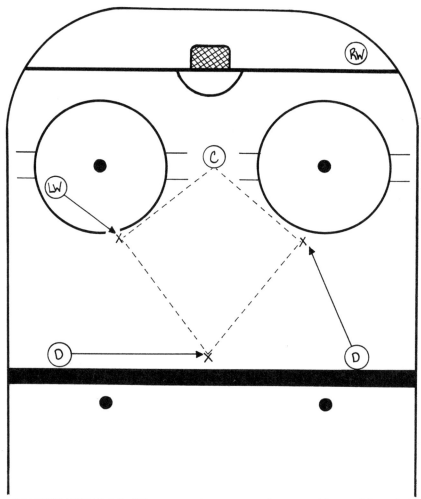

ILLUSTRATION 4-3. *When one player goes down and is unable to join the play, the other attackers must be willing to shift their positions to plug any open holes.*

When this happens, the offensive player who is away from the play will help plug a second hole now opened by the other defenseman as he skates to center ice at the blue line to attempt to cover both point areas. The forward now becomes a temporary defenseman until a balanced attack can be reestablished.

If a forward has some unusual talent, like being very large and strong or having extremely quick hands, the coach may try to play him in a slightly different offensive position on the ice in order to capitalize on the other team's weaknesses. For example, the coach

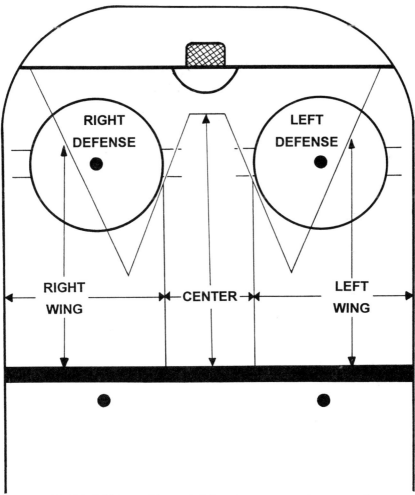

ILLUSTRATION 4-4. *Normal defensive zone assignments for a defensive team.*

may try to have a wing and center switch offensive ice positions so that the dominant player on one team is challenging either the dominant player or the weakest player on the other team. Or the coach may have his best defensive forward "shadow" the opponent's best offensive player around the ice wherever he travels. To shadow a player means to have one player follow an opponent, usually the best player, everywhere on the ice that the player skates. Many times, the shadow will literally drape himself all over the player being shadowed and will be a general nuisance. The object is to prevent this outstanding player from being as effective as he would be if left to his own devices. There is no set strategy for matching up players against opponents, but we will present some basic strategies and approaches here. A shadow needs to have perseverance and a high tolerance for punishment, and be a great skater.

In the defensive zone, the wings will skate as necessary either backward or alongside of the attacking wing, confronting or defending against the opposing wings as they enter the zone. The defensive forwards attempt to establish their presence along the boards in the same general vicinity that they patrol offensively. The center will follow along with the puck, skating in an inverted umbrella pattern, fanning out along the blue line and narrowing the defensive zone as it backs toward the goal. Often times, the center will also hook around behind the goal to present a flooded zone and be able to assist his teammates in gaining control of the puck.

When control of the puck is established, depending on which player has gained control, the forwards will generally relinquish control of the puck to one of the defensemen while still in the defensive zone. This defenseman will usually be an offensive defenseman who will start the charge out of the zone with the puck while the offensive players break into position toward neutral ice and help divert straggling opponents away from the approaching play. When the attack is formulated, as the defenseman crosses his own blue line, he will forward pass the puck to a breaking forward at the red line, usually the center, and then trail behind the play in case it goes awry. The forwards who do not have the puck will continue to attempt to draw the opposing players away from the forming play or the puck carrier. So again, forwards are playing defense as well as offense, and are playing it in all three zones on the ice, not just one.

CENTERS

To borrow a term from football, the center is the "quarterback" of the team. The responsibility of the center is first to put the puck into play by participating in and winning a face-off. A face-off is when two opposing centers face each other as the referee drops a puck between their waiting sticks. As the puck hits the ice, each player immediately tries to sweep it into his defensive zone to one of his own teammates so his team can gain control. Once control is established, the team can then set an up offensive attack. The battle for control of the puck is often rough and physical, so a center needs to have great forearm and wrist strength.

When taking a face-off, the center needs uncanny anticipation. He must be ready with the tip of his stick blade on the ice at

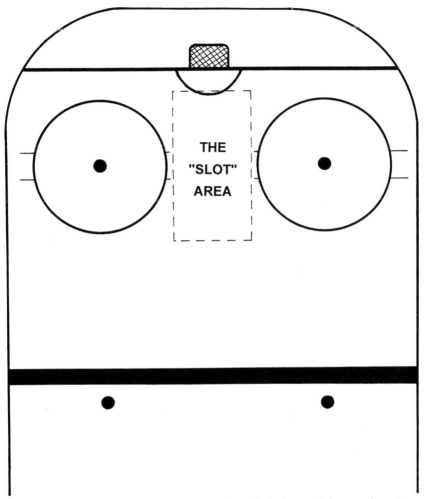

ILLUSTRATION 4-5. *The slot area directly in front of the goaltender is highly fought over because of its high scoring possibilities.*

his feet. Hands are low on the shaft, wrists are loose. His eyes are concentrating on the face-off dot and nothing else. As he sees the puck enter his vision from above, he begins the move of his stick across the ice toward the other player to block off the opponent's stick while at the same time trying to scoop the puck back into his own zone toward a teammate. The center cannot let anything distract him from performing this important duty. One missed face-off can cost the team the game, especially late in the third period. With this type of pressure, a center also needs nerves of steel.

A center should be a strong player, especially in the legs and

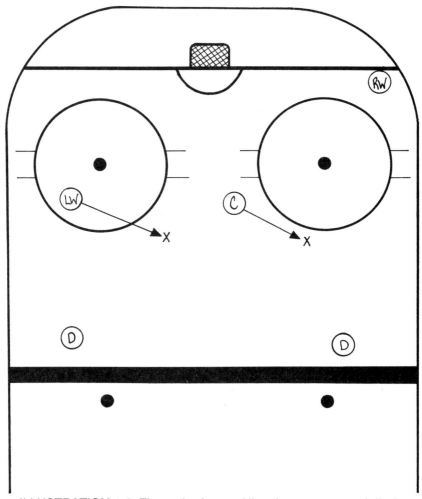

ILLUSTRATION 4-6. *The entire forward line, but most especially the center, must be flexible and willing to fill in where needed in an instant.*

upper arms. He must be a good skater with good hands. He doesn't need to be an extremely fast skater (but most are). He will often lead and direct the play into the offensive zone and the play will develop around him. Centers do not necessarily need to be physically big. Usually, a center is a smallish, wiry kind of player who can dig himself easily into and out of tight situations. On offense, the center will patrol the center ice area high in the slot looking for a pass to come to him. He will maneuver up and down through the area—constantly moving—looking to get open.

When not involved directly in the play at the puck, the center will attempt to distract and tie up one of the opposing defensemen to take him out of the play, not by physical interference but by being a constantly swarming pest darting in and out of the goal area. In addition, when a wing is taken out of the play or is caught too deep in a corner, a center will skate laterally slightly to cover the territory opened by the absence of the wing. This position is only temporary until the wing can recover. It is very important that the center stay aware of the openings created by the absences of the other players. He needs good coverage ability.

Because a center needs to be able to receive a pass and control the puck at all times, the best centers have an innate ability to keep their sticks down on the ice under even the most strenuous situations. A good center can keep his stick poised for a pass or tip-in even when he finds himself draped by an opposing defenseman. Centers need lightning-quick reflexes. The puck can be passed or deflected to them at any time—it may come deliberately from a teammate or accidentally from an opposing player or even off the goalie in a rebound. Centers need the ability to gain control of the puck and fire in on the net quickly and accurately.

For all these reasons, a center needs unswerving concentration, a good hockey sense, and good peripheral vision. As he usually is the one to carry the puck into the offensive zone to make the play, he will have huge defensemen bearing down on him, trying to strip him of the puck and plaster him onto the ice. He rarely will be coming down on the wing with the boards to his back and usually will be skating in open center ice. A center needs to be able to see the whole ice surface, and know where all the other players on both teams are at all times. A center needs a sixth sense as he may need to pass off left or right in a split second; may drop pass to a trailing wing or defenseman behind him; may need to know when to dump the puck into the zone or when to break away from a play that may get him into trouble defensively.

A center needs to have "soft" hands. This means that the shots a center takes will probably not be very hard shots; in fact, many of the attempts will be made with finesse. They will be difficult and delicate shots. The center often scores on redirection shots from the point (tip-ins), shovel shots into tight openings off rebounds, and little flip backhand shots over the fallen goaltender. In order to be able to *take* these chances, he has to be able to *make* these chances, and he makes these chances by being "in the way" of incoming shots, creating havoc, and being a general nuisance to the other team. In short, the center needs to be able to handle the pressure to be the nucleus of the team.

WINGS

The left and right wings usually are bigger and stronger players than centers. Coaches are discovering that one small wing on a line can often prove very effective. The smaller player is able to dig deeper into corners with less difficulty and can usually come away from the skirmish with the puck. This is not, however, the rule of lineup formation; it is the exception. If you have a small wing, the player needs to be powerful, dominant, and controlling. This type of player is very rare. Left and right wings need to be strong, fast skaters as they often will find themselves catching up to the play in the neutral zone as it is forming around the center. Wings need to have excellent maneuverability with both feet and hands. It is the wings who go crashing head first into the corners against the opposing defensemen and it is the wings who dig for the puck. This ferocious action often gets shuffled back behind the net where the ice between the boards and the rear of the net is only twelve feet wide. Wings need agile feet to kick the puck along, and good hand and arm strength to dig for long periods of time in the corners.

A wing needs to be able to receive a puck passed to him while he is on the fly, moving quickly down the wing and breaking toward the net. Wings also need excellent passing ability. The wing is often the one behind the net looking for the open player driving toward the goal. In another instance, the wing may be skating into the zone at full speed while carrying the puck and suddenly need to produce a cross-ice pass to the other wing as they work together to draw opposing players out of the play. Because wings are often trapped between burly defensemen and the hard boards, they need to be big and strong and prepared to take—and deliver—punishment.

Wings should have an excellent shot, especially from the top of the face-off circles. They usually have to take slapshots on the fly as they cross over the blue line. Wings should practice high speed shots whenever possible. Many times a wing will be caught in or asked to play the "off wing." This means he will be playing the wing opposite his normal wing. This can have adverse effects on a player if he tries to play in his normal fashion. On a player's usual wing, the back of his stick blade and the back of his body are against the boards and he is facing the action as he skates down the boards. On the off wing, the open curve of the stick is facing the boards and the player's back is facing the play.

The player is forced to take passes on the backhand, a very difficult position from which to make the transition to forehand to get off shots. It forces the player to stop, pivot open, and then head directly toward or shoot for the net. Because of the stop, there is a bit of extra time for opponents to either get into position to defend against the shot or to check the wing off the puck. A player has to be very strong and have the skating ability to pull off this maneuver. He also needs a quick, low, and hard shot from this ice position. The wing will often be the offensive player to take the initial opening shot attempt in an offensive drive hoping for a clean goal or to create a rebound. This shot must be a good one. The wing's ability to make goals cannot be overemphasized.

DEFENSEMEN

Defensive Responsibilities

The primary role of the defense is to help prevent goals. Notice I did not say to stop goals, as that job lies with the goaltender. It is the responsibility of the defensemen to clear out stray rebounds and to help give the goaltender an equal and clear chance to stop the shots as they are launched toward the net. The goaltender needs uninterrupted concentration to perform his job to the best of his ability. It is the task of the defensive players to make sure that the goaltender is given the opportunity to concentrate.

The defensemen accomplish this by clearing the zone directly in front of the goal, known as the slot, by removing any opponents who might be cruising the slot area looking for a pass or rebound. As it is illegal to interfere with a player who does not have the puck, the task of removing lingering offensive players becomes tricky. Defensive players can accomplish this through various means. They can simply stand and cruise in the slot themselves, taking up room and making themselves "big" by spreading out arms and stick so that offensive players have little room to move easily. The defense must know how to make themselves "small" in an instant even before the shot approaches as this action may block the vision of the goaltender.

A team's key to an effective and controlling defense is to have set defensive pairs. Pairs are two defensive players who are assigned to play with each other at all times. Defensive partners must work in harmony and unison with each other because there are only two defensemen covering three rushing forwards in the defensive zone with limited help from the offense. Each defensive partner must know where the other is at all times.

A defensive pair often will consist of a very defensive-minded player, known as a "stay-at-home" defenseman and an offensive-minded player, known as a "rushing" defenseman. One player is often big and dominating defensively while the other is smaller, but still strong and with good puckhandling ability. As the two players work together on defensive shifts in both practice and in games,

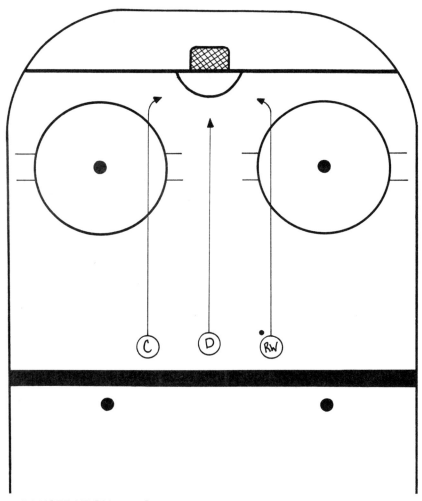

ILLUSTRATION 4-7. *On a two-on-one breakaway, the defenseman needs to stay between the two attackers to cut off any passes and to allow the goalie a fair chance to stop the shot.*

they need to communicate both on and off the ice discussing which areas each will cover in certain situations. For example, if the puck goes behind the net on a "dump-in," they both can't go for it and leave the defensive zone unprotected in front of the goalie. They need to work out in advance who will retrieve the puck and who will guard the zone. Usually the better stick-handler will retrieve the puck. On two-on-two and three-on-two breakaways, they must have a set plan of defense. They must determine who will take the puck carrier and who will cover the other attacker or skaters. If both or neither cover the puck carrier, a disaster surely will occur.

The puck carrier is usually covered by the defenseman whose side he is on. When a coach finds a defensive pair who work well together, he should try hard not to break up that pair.

In normal situations, the defense will approach puckhandlers and carriers as they enter the zone and attempt to force them off toward the boards. This opens up the slot area for the goalie to see. On two-on-one breakaways, a single defenseman attempts to take the non-puck carrier out of the play by getting between the two attacking offensive players to eliminate a pass, all while drifting backward toward the puck carrier to harass or distract him. Although this lets the puck carrier come in alone on the goaltender, it gives the goalie a fair chance to stop a clean shot and it also prevents a pass off to the open player.

Another responsibility of the defensemen is to clear the zone of the puck. In some defensive systems, the defensemen will be assigned to always play the puck instead of the man. That is, they will go for the puck whenever it is in their defensive area while their partner goes for the man. The first defenseman simply will dump the puck out of the zone or clear it off to one side for a teammate to recover when it is either loose in the area or is picked off while coming in on net. The second defenseman always will check the carrier while his partner worries about the puck.

When an offensive play is not established in the zone by the attacking team, the role of the defenseman is to help break up any organization the offensive team may have, gain control of the puck, and begin then to turn the play around toward the other end of the ice. A defenseman accomplishes this by digging hard in the corners and behind the net against the opposing team's wings, attempting to gain control of the puck or at least to prevent the other team from gaining control.

The final defensive responsibility is to know how, when, and where to freeze the puck to force a face-off. There will be many times throughout the course of a game that because of unusual circumstances—such as the puck bouncing free or the offensive team flooding an area; no team being able to gain substantial control; play getting too uncontrollable; or an imminent danger of a goal being scored—where the defenseman cannot let the game continue and must force the play to stop. This is accomplished in a variety of ways. If the play is in the crease and the defenseman cannot clear the crease of either the puck or opposing players, he may tuck the puck under the goaltender's glove, pads, or fallen body to freeze it. Usually the goalie will see this action coming and help out by pressing his body hard to the ice. The defenseman must still take care not to shove too hard or else the puck will move under the goalie's outstretched body into his own net. It is best to try to shove it under the goalie's glove. It is a penalty for the defenseman alone to freeze the puck in the crease. Only the goalie can freeze the puck in the net mouth. Make sure that the goalie is clearly in the crease before you attempt to freeze the puck there.

Two opposing players may legally freeze the puck against the side boards. It is a penalty for one player to stop play for no reason. If two opponents are attempting to freeze the puck simultaneously, this is a legal maneuver. The defense may legally freeze the puck against the side boards with the willing help of an opposing player. This is accomplished by placing the skate flat sideways, flush against the boards with the puck trapped between the skate blade and the boards.

The final way to freeze a puck is one that few players will want to try on a regular basis as it involves stopping a fired puck with their body while sliding into the shot lying on their side and wrapping themselves around the puck while down on the ice to force the face-off. As this is a *very dangerous* procedure, I do not recommend it for youth hockey. It takes a lot of skill and timing practice to get this process just right. The end result of a forced face-off is just not worth the risk of injury. Coaches, please do not let your players perform this maneuver.

Offensive Contributions

In a perfect world, all defensemen would have to worry about would be preventing scoring chances and helping block goals. But that's not the case. The defense must contribute offensively as well.

The offensive attack is first conceived in the defensive zone by the defense as a defensive player gains control of the puck and starts the offensive rush toward center ice. The play's execution is begun by the defense's accurate passing of the puck to the breaking forwards as they hit center ice at full stride. As the action shifts up ice, the play is then secured by the defense clearing out the trailing zone and shoring up the trailing blue line, preventing opposing players from drifting back into the zone. Subsequent to the play entering the attack zone, it develops in the offensive zone as the defensemen act as control gates (also known as point men) at the blue line to keep the play alive. The play succeeds as the offense launches the puck toward the goal for a tip-in or score!

The role of the defenseman in the offense cannot be overstated. As the game is played today, the defensive players are as important to the offense in helping to score goals as they are to the defense in preventing them. As a coach, I used to insist that my defensemen play "D" and leave the scoring to those whose job it is to score. I realized my thinking was out-of-date, and changed my coaching strategies. I became more aware that the defensemen are an integral part of an effective offense. The defensemen became the final two figures, the trailing forwards as it were, in the offensive formula. No longer do the defensemen sit on their own blue line and wait for the opposing team to start back on a rush. The defense is up in the offensive zone—involved in digging for the puck, taking control of the offense, and, sometimes, leading the charge.

As the game has developed over time, coaches have realized that not only is it important to have two big, strong players on defense to clear the zone with a dump pass or to knock down players, they have learned how essential it is to have a player who can bring the puck out of the zone and kick-start the offense. When a coach has such a play-maker stranded behind the blue line, he is wasting a valuable offensive talent.

To better understand the role of the modern defenseman, we need to examine a defensive history. The role and face of the defenseman changed radically in the early '70s. Bobby Orr, famous defenseman for the Boston Bruins, coaches' thinking for all time. With exceptional skating skills, superior puckhandling ability, accurate shooting, and a good sense of command, he became the captain of the charge on the ice. The Bruins would funnel the puck to him deep in the defensive zone and he would initiate his now famous end-to-end rushes right alongside the offense. Having an Orr is like having a fourth forward.

As with any change in procedure, there were disadvantages to this style of play. One such detriment was having Orr's defensive partner left hanging in the zone without backup in the event the play went awry. Opposing coaches quickly observed the weakness created by this gap and learned to capitalize on the opportunity that was opened for them. They would also double and triple team Orr as he rushed the puck to wear him down throughout the game. Players would hit him hard and often.

In spite of this, Orr still accepted every opportunity to carry the puck, and he opened his own door to get hit. Knowing this, coaches explicitly instructed their players to dump the puck toward Orr's area in the zone so he would carry the puck. As he moved the puck out of his zone, opposing coaches instructed their players to focus in on Orr, to make him and him alone the target of their aggression and hit him at every opportunity. This keen strategy soon began to take its toll on the talented young player. His knees were the first to go. His back soon followed, his superstar career was soon over. But in twelve NHL seasons with Boston and later with Chicago, this Hall of Fame player played in 657 games and accumulated 915 points! Orr is the example of the effectiveness of a rushing defenseman. Coaches had to devise whole new strategies to stop just one player. Since Bobby Orr, every defenseman is expected to be part offenseman.

Obviously, the "D" no longer needs to limit itself to behind the blue line. There are many offensive contributions that can be made by the defense. In addition to the example provided by Orr, the defenseman's main offensive contributions are to remain on or near the blue line in the offensive zone, keep the puck in the zone and in play, and act as the point man. The point man is a player, usually a defenseman with a strong and accurate slapshot, who cruises a few feet in front of the offensive blue line in the attack zone. The player covers ice from his own boards out along the blue line to slightly beyond center ice. As the point man, a defenseman needs to be a good, quick skater. As the play formulates deep in the offensive zone and draws the opposing team's players away from the blue line toward it, the puck is fired out to the point man for a one-timer or even for possible regrouping. A one-timer is a quick hard shot taken immediately by the point man as the puck reaches his location. The player does not wait until the puck gets to him to set it up for the shot. He sees the puck coming to him from either out of the pack or from the other point man, and begins his wind-up for the shot as it still is approaching him. As the puck slides into location at the point man's feet, the defenseman fires the puck with perfect timing and without stopping his motion. The advantages to this play are enormous. The shot comes off quickly and opposing players do not have time to react to it. The flow of the play may be moving in the opposite direction to the puck. It sets up excellent tip-in opportunities and there are plenty of chances for deflections.

A play like this, executed perfectly, usually results in a goal. Therein lies the problem—"executed perfectly." This is an extremely difficult maneuver to master. Timing is everything. If the point man misses the puck, it will go skittering into the neutral zone breaking up the play. If he doesn't strike the puck cleanly and it's wobbling along the ice, it can easily be picked off by an opposing player. A defenseman needs to have many talents to pull this off: ice-covering ability, excellent balance, a tremendous shot, and a lot of confidence. If a player works on these skills, all other skills will fall into place. By concentrating on these particulars, a player is also working on his shot, his passing ability, his skating, his defensive ability, and his all-around game. From the point position, the defenseman can help control the offense, set up plays, and control the flow of the game.

As a coach, I still do not let my defensive players get too deep into the attack zone. I feel that they need to master defense first or else they should move to offense. It is better for a defenseman to have excellent defensive abilities and weaker offensive skills than the other way around. Once they have proven defensive ability, let them then try to improve their offensive skills.

GOALTENDERS

The primary duty of the goaltender (keep, netminder, goalie) is to stop the puck from going into the net by any means and at any cost within the rules. Complete methods and specific skills necessary for the goalie to know will be discussed in detail in Chapter 6, but for illustrative purposes, some basic skills and requirements for the goalie will be introduced here.

Basic Responsibilities

A goalie needs to be athletic. The goalie always begins his duties in the net in a crouch facing the play. This is the basic starting position for all goalies. As the play advances up and down and across the lanes on the ice, the goalie shifts laterally back and forth across the crease in front of the play so that as much of him as possible is between the puck and the net at all times. A goalie needs excellent skating skills and quick lateral movement across the mouth of the goal. With this shifting maneuver, the goalie is able to be ready for the play at all times. As the play is approaching the goalie, either as a clean breakaway or with defenders interfering, the goalie begins to move forward in the crease out of the goal mouth to the top of the crease or slightly beyond. By "cutting down the angle," the shooters see less net to shoot at and the goalie appears bigger.

I tell the defense at all times a goalie cannot stop a shot he cannot see. The goalie needs to have a good view of the ice and know where the puck is at all times. If the defense does not screen the goalie or does not allow the goaltender to be screened, then it is the goalie's responsibility to see and stop the initial shot. A good netminder will also help limit rebounds back out onto the offensive playing surface. When stopping or blocking the shot, he will attempt to direct the puck either away from the goal and out to a teammate or down to the ice at his own knees where he can control the puck himself. After the initial stop of the puck, depending on where defenders and teammates are, the goalie may either shove the puck around back of the net if the area is clear, allow a teammate to scoop it up and skate off with it, or fall on the puck to freeze it if danger is imminent.

A goalie also needs to be brave. It is a scary proposition to a little person to be asked to put his body on the line to stop a puck. A goalie needs a lot of confidence in his equipment and himself. It

This goalie is facing a lot of problems. He is turned away from the play, he is down on his knees, and his glove and stick are not ready. He needs to learn to return quickly to his ready crouch.

takes a lot of faith on the goalie's part to realize that, for the most part, the puck really will not hurt that much when it hits him. The goalie is so well-protected the sting of the shot is minimized if not absent. This is not to say that there won't be cases where the puck sneaks in behind some pads and finds some flesh. When this happens, it hurts! But for the most part, the goalie needs a lot of confidence in his equipment plus a little bit of bravery.

Additional Responsibilities

Earlier, we discussed Bobby Orr's role in the reshaping of the defense. Another current player has had a similar impact on the perceived role of the netminder. Ron Hextall of the New York Islanders showed during his tenure with the Philadelphia Flyers that the goalie need not stay planted in his crease. Hextall was the first goalie to ever actually score a goal by shooting the puck into the opposing team's net from his own end, and he did it not once but twice! Hextall has revolutionized the goaltender's stick-handling chores and abilities. A tremendous skater and very confident puck-handler, he takes control of the puck as it is dumped into his zone and can act as a third defenseman on the ice by jumpstarting the offense. He gets the puck back up the ice very quickly, long before

Here the goalie is making himself "big"; he's trying to plug all the holes and spread himself out to stop any rebound shots.

the offense has had time to vacate the zones completely and retreat back into their own end to regroup.

This trend of a stick-handling goalie is filtering down to even the youngest levels, as the little players with impressionable minds watch their heroes perform on television. Hextall also gets into a lot of trouble by getting too far out of his net and by getting too fancy with his stick. But he has excellent goaltending skills to help cover for his mistakes. In emulating Hextall, youngsters often find they have bitten off more than they can chew, trying to balance solid goaltending abilities with stick-handling skills. Unless you are the professional who has worked on these techniques for years, one aspect of your game will suffer. It has taken Hextall many, many years to perfect his talents and skills. I still prefer that my goalies stay within ten yards of the net at all times, and let the defense control the puck at first opportunity but I've been wrong before. The future could well be that a goalie needs to be an excellent stick-handler, but I won't go that far right now. I'll just say that a goalie needs to be comfortable handling the puck around his own net and be fairly adept at passing the puck while wearing those awkward gloves. Maybe as the players get older and gain confidence and maturity, I'll reconsider my thinking. Until that time, I'll stick with a solid defensive goaltender.

A goalie must be cool and calm under pressure. He must be able to analyze the situation and respond immediately. A goalie who panics does not stay in the nets for long. After the initial stop of the puck, play doesn't always unfold the way a goalie would prefer it to. The puck may rapidly rebound out to an opponent so a goalie needs quick reflexes and an ability to make himself "big," especially when lying flat on the ice. This is not a new concept as defensemen employ this tactic as well. Making yourself big entails spreading out your arms, leg pads, stick, and glove across the opening of the net while keeping the body holes plugged.

A goalie needs excellent agility. After the initial stop of the puck, a goalie needs to be able to get back onto his skates quickly, regain composure, and set up again for the next barrage which may come anywhere from a few seconds to a few minutes later, depending on what his teammates do with the puck. The movement of the puck by the defense also depends somewhat on the goalie. After the goalie's team has regained possession of the puck, it is the netminder's duty to help direct offensive traffic out of the zone. Because he can see all of the ice, the astute and alert goalie should shout out directions to his teammates. He should let them know where opponents are; if the opposing players are coming in on the puck and his defensemen may not see or be aware of their movement; if teams are changing shifts; and any other information regarding what is occurring out on the ice. This is especially true if the player corralling the puck has his back to the play or if opponents have sneaked their way in behind a player advancing the puck out of the zone. A goalie needs a good set of lungs and a loud voice, and must not be afraid to use them.

Classic goalies cannot be shy on the ice. They need to be aggressive. When the puck is dumped in the zone from down the ice, the netminder must go out and get it. If the puck is losing steam as it crosses the blue line, the goalie must skate up to it, corral it, and send it back quickly to a teammate who is retreating to pick it up. He must do all of this while watching oncoming opponents and his own net. If the puck is fired in hard on a "wrap-around," the goalie must skate out around back of the net in the opposite direction of the traveling puck and stop it so a teammate can collect it. The goalie must always be aware of the location of all opponents and the puck.

A goalie cannot be rushing out to challenge shooters to force their moves prematurely—especially on breakaways. He must wait for the shooter to make the first move. If neither player wavers first, the goalie will always win the shootout. A goalie should not initiate his movement to stop the puck until the puck is moving toward him. In other words, he should not physically anticipate what

When possible, it is the goalie's job to cut off the wrap-around and set up the puck for a teammate.

he thinks the shooter will do until the puck has actually been fired by the attacker. If the goalie makes the first move, the shooter will counteract and may score. For example, if the goalie thinks the shot will be hit high and he moves his glove up and high, a good shooter will take advantage of this movement and shoot low for the score. A goalie must be patient and have nerves of steel.

A goalie also needs patience when sitting the bench. No one player can play every minute of every game. Most teams carry at least two goaltenders. On my bantam team, I rotate the goalies, letting each play every other game regardless of what happened in the previous game. Two sets of parents are paying a lot of money to watch their children play hockey, and they will play. Of course, if one goalie doesn't show up, then the other plays again, but usually they are willing to alternate goalkeeping assignments. So a goalie needs to be a good team player as well.

A goalie needs to be able to take direction. The coach may call in the netminder after a poor period or two and explain that he is just not looking right out there, maybe looking a little shaky or confused, and it may be time for a change of goalies. Maybe the coach needs to shake his team up a little and put some fire under his players. A coach may change goalies just to accomplish this and ignite that fire. This is nothing personal against the goalie, and the player needs to understand this. So a goalie needs to be cooperative as well. Goalies also need to be cheerleaders from the bench. They must have the right attitude and ability to motivate the team on the ice or in the locker room while they themselves are "sitting the wood."

Finally, when the game is over, win or lose, the goalie must have a personality that can take pressure and responsibility and can allow criticism to roll off his back. It's never easy to accept a loss, but the goalie cannot allow the burden of the loss to be placed solely on him. Even if the game was 20 to 0, it is not entirely the goalie's fault. Hockey is a team sport, and with a score like that, obviously the whole team was playing below its potential. The youngster who was the netminder must learn that nothing he would have or could have done, even standing on his head, would have changed the outcome of the game. Even if he let up only one goal, that alone would not have been enough to win. No one person can carry a team. Even the best goalie in the world can't do it.

The responsibilities of the goalie are directly related to the demeanor that he needs to carry out his duties effectively. The team and coach need a goalie who will help them in their efforts to win, not hinder them. A goalie helps a team to win by being the best possible team player.

We will discuss more specific goaltending skills later, but until then, coaches and parents have an idea of what kind of player can be a goalie. A goalie is unlike any other player on the ice.

So now the coach has all the players in the positions that suit their styles of play and personalities. Each player has agreed to play his position to the best of his ability. Each knows what to do in his position and how to accomplish and complete his role on the team. There is one small problem that remains however. What specific skills should each player practice and what does each player actually do when on the ice? How does this group of twenty-two individuals become a team? Keep practicing—a team is a unified body of players with established practiced plays, which utilizes these plays within a game to produce a win. In the next chapter, we will look at some very basic plays and procedures that all hockey players need to know before getting started playing the game. Get your clipboards and chalkboards ready. Here we go.

5.

GAME PLAY IN ACTION—
TEAM SKILLS

The American Heritage Dictionary, Second College Edition defines hockey as, "A game played on the ice in which two opposing teams of skaters, using curved sticks, try to drive a puck into the opponents' goal." It defines team as, "A group on the same side, as in a game," and "A group organized to work together." Notice that the definition of hockey specifies "teams of skaters," and not individuals or single players.

Skaters "organized to work together." That's what it's all about. That's what we're all on the ice to do—to organize our group of individual wayfarers into a sleek skating team of players. It is in knowing, understanding, and following these two definitions that we begin this section. I cannot stress enough that the group of twenty-two individuals, the group that we didn't know what to do with, the group of haphazardly put together players, is now a team, and as a team must begin to work together toward a common goal. *Individuals* do not play the game of hockey, but they are part of the team that plays the game.

To get the individuals playing like a team, you as the coach must introduce the concept of teamwork. To many players, especially to the young players who have never played organized sports before, this is an innovative and strange concept. Players are no longer playing for their own private glory or pleasure. They are playing for the distinction and the triumph of other teammates.

Developing his team feeling takes a kind of maturity that probably has not been expected of these youngsters up to this point in their lives.

TEAMBUILDING DRILLS

It is actually not as difficult as it sounds to instill and practice the principles of teamwork. To make the concept of teamwork blossom within a game is another thing. The team already has passing and skating drills to work on, but now it needs teamwork skills exercises. An excellent introductory exercise that helps to demonstrate the importance of teamwork is what I refer to as the "One plus one plus ..." exercise.

One Plus One Plus ...

Begin by giving one player the puck at the end boards behind the goal line. It is that player's responsibility to carry the puck up the ice and shoot it into the goal. Of course, that's too easy with just empty ice and an empty net. So, place all the rest of the team players scattered equally about on the ice facing the on-rushing player and just for fun include both goalies in the goal. The team players cannot leave the zone to which they are assigned, but can go anywhere in that zone. Using any legal means, it is their job to stop the rushing player and strip him of the puck.

Of course, as the player begins to move out, no matter which direction he takes, he will be met with considerable resistance, and very likely won't get too far. After his attempt is halted, take any one other player from the on-ice squad and reassign him as a "teammate" of the single rusher. The two players together then try to make it up ice. They can skate, pass, or carry the puck as they wish. Of course, together they probably won't make it very far, but they might make it a little further than the first attempt. After each stoppage, repeat the process by taking one player off the defending team and moving him to the offensive team. The sides will soon begin to balance out and the time will come when one of the rushing players makes it through the line and shoots for the goal. Of course, there will still be two goalies to contend with but they, too, will be defeated with time and additional players. Continue with the exercise until the entire team has shifted from defenders to rushers. Before long, the "team" will quickly begin to realize and experience firsthand how teamwork pays off.

For a coach, this example will go a long way in the locker room to serve to emphasize your point. It is an excellent example of teamwork, and how one player just cannot do it alone—no matter how much skill he has. As the team grows, the task becomes more manageable. As the team betters itself, the job becomes more realistic. As the team develops, the chore becomes easier. Finally, there is no longer an obstacle to scoring, because the team is working together to get past the defenders, and has the proficiency, capability, and desire to accomplish the feat.

One aside: As a coach, you may encounter an occasionally player who manages to make it through the gauntlet once in a while as a lone individual. Needless to say, keep an eye on that player! He has either tremendous talent and skill, or very devious skating and stick-handling abilities. This player could be either a superstar, big trouble, or maybe even both. Choose carefully the players you shift from one team to the other and try to keep talent balanced. If you make things too lop-sided or uneven, the players will know you're trying to pull a "fast one" on them and won't see and reap the benefits of the exercise. You may even want to start out with the "best" player, or a hothead, or someone who thinks he can do it all. The entire team will soon learn that no one, not the best, nor the biggest, nor the smartest player can do it without teammates.

Keep-Away

Another teamwork building skill to practice includes a passing game of keep-away. This is essentially opposite of the "One plus one plus ..." rushing game. With players scattered about the ice, one player tries to take the puck away from the team as the team passes it around. Of course, this is a near impossible task for just one defender. Any one passing player cannot hold onto the puck for more than five seconds. Coaches should be counting out loud. After thirty seconds have elapsed with one or more players chasing the puck, the coach blows a whistle and the player who presently has control of the puck (or if the puck is between two players, the last player to touch the puck) moves over to the chasing team. Continue this exercise as above until you have depleted the keeping team. Soon, the players will see this task can only be completed with teamwork. Soon, any player can take commanding control of the puck as a result of employing teamwork. One player can't play keep-away by himself; you need a "team" to play.

This is also a great exercise to use to work on team passing skills, so it can be employed in more than one scenario to teach the players about both passing and cooperation.

Natural Leaders

It's interesting, as either the rushing team in the first exercise or the chasing team in the second exercise "grows," the players begin to take it upon themselves to develop plans of attack and action to follow that help them maximize their efforts to succeed in their goal. Coaches, I feel it is essential to note which players take on the responsibility and leadership roles in these situations and then carry through these roles and show they are able to demonstrate their leadership skills. Also note which players try to bully themselves into leadership positions in the group. These team leaders, both the good and the bad, may eventually go on, for better or for worse, to become your team captains.

It also provides you with the opportunity to see which players may need to be given the opening to lead when the time comes to select team leaders. For example, the players you think are good leaders may not be loud or outgoing enough to be known to the entire team. The quiet player would probably prefer to lead by example and actions rather than by words. This may be just the type of captain your team needs to lead it on the ice. In addition, if the team is a new team and the players are unfamiliar with each other, these exercises give them an opportunity to work together and find a natural rhythm together.

It is important to emphasize that teamwork is not something that you can *give* to your players. It can only be earned, cultivated, and grown within the team by the players themselves. Yet without it, a team can neither function nor exist and it certainly cannot excel. The game of hockey, which everyone at the rink and in the locker room loves so dearly, cannot be played without teamwork.

There is another almost contradictory element that should also be stressed to your players. In spite of appearances, however, it by no means goes against the principles of teamwork. A major task of the coach is also to make your players know, feel, and understand that each of them is a vital and important cog in the wheel of the team. By any means possible, get your players to understand that the team exists and succeeds because of everyone's individual skills, personal hard work, particular desires and ambition, working within the framework of the team. That it is their individuality working together as a team unit that leads to accomplishment, achievement, conquest, and, ultimately, victory. Stress to each player that he or she is a vital and important part of the team, and without each one, no matter how young or small of stature, the team cannot exist. In essence, don't just make each player *feel* important, make each one *be* important. Make everyone a part of the team. As a good coach, you must find a role for each of your players, even if it's just a small role.

Goals

Establish individual and team goals for each player. These goals may be simple or elaborate. One player may have a personal goal to score three goals this season, or to make three good checks a game, or maybe even just to show up on the ice on time for each practice. Let the players know that you are interested in each of

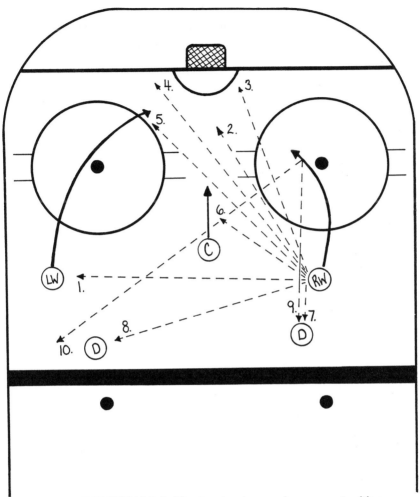

ILLUSTRATION 5-1. *The ten basic passing opportunities open to any offensive player as he enters the attack zone to set up a scoring chance.*

them as an individual, and that you are willing to do whatever you can to work together with them to better their skills and help them become better overall players. After all, that is the job of a coach.

BASIC PASSING OPPORTUNITIES

Before we even begin to discuss offensive scoring plays, every player on the ice must know and understand all of the options of basic passing and the scoring opportunities that are open upon entering the offensive zone. Every player needs not only to know

ILLUSTRATION 5-2. *An offensive line should cross the blue line
staggered when carrying the puck to avoid going offsides.
The puck carrier must be the lead skater.*

where to pass, but also where and when he might receive a pass.
He needs to be able to place himself in the correct position on the
ice to be open to present the puckhandler the opportunity to pass
to him if warranted. The following simple diagram will present all
of the pass-making and pass-receiving opportunities available to
each offensive team player upon entering the zone.

Study the diagram and see what opportunities you can identify in it before I give you the answers. We'll get back to the diagram in just a little bit. Once the basic passing opportunities are

committed to memory, the team can initiate its basic attack skills. On the basic attack, the offensive line enters the zone slightly staggered. Any alternate configuration of the players is permitted (right or left wing carrying or center carrying), but the puck carrier is always the leading player and the non-puck carriers are always slightly trailing.

The four rules, in order of importance, that each player must remember are these:

1. Always shoot first to the *open* net. (An open net is still guarded by the goalie but loosely protected or not guarded by the defense.)

2. If the net is not open, pass to an open man.

3. When in doubt, if there is no open man, shoot toward the net and then break toward it for a rebound.

4. When in apparent trouble, dump the puck to an open off-corner (one not being protected) and retreat to regroup.

I tell my players over and over and over again. Shoot, shoot, shoot, *shoot*! No one can score unless he shoots the puck! When desperate for more shots on goal, I play a little game with my players. Every player (except goalies) must take at least two legitimate shots on goal in a game. For every player who does not take his two required shots, that neglect translates to two extra wind sprints the length of the rink at practice. The first time they thought I was kidding. Boy, did they ever discover how wrong they were when they had to skate the sprints ten times! Five guys didn't take even a single shot. Amazingly after that first time, they began to shoot more for the net and before long, I had every player gunning for the net. We started getting forty to fifty shots a game instead of ten to twelve shots on goal as we had been getting. If a team is consistently scoring on less than ten percent of its shots, (e.g., 14 shots on goal = 1 goal) then it only stands to reason that the more shots the team takes, the more goals it will score (e.g., 34 shots on goal = 3 goals). That's exactly how it worked out. We had the talent to do it. We went from averaging one goal a game to over three goals a game. We won some of those games as well, but even in a loss, the kids felt better about themselves because they all were contributing to the successes of the team, not just two or three scorers.

Referring back to Illustration 5-1, the ten basic passing opportunities presented to the puckhandler are as follows (We will assume that the puckhandler is the right wing. Obviously, the identity and location of the puck carrier will change the passing opportunities.):

1. Cross ice to the opposite wing
2. Up to the slot
3. At the left side of the goalie
4. At the right side of the goalie
5. To the crashing wing
6. To the crashing center
7. Drop to the trailing defenseman
8. Across ice to the opposite defenseman
9. In and back to the right point
10. In and back to the left point

Knowing these passing opportunities will get many players out of trouble and many other players into scoring chances without their having to give up the puck in the zone. The puck carrier doesn't even need to be an excellent puckhandler or passer to make these passes work, as long as there will be someone on the other end of the pass. They don't require "thread the needle" passing or fancy behind the back and between the legs stick-handling. These are basic plays that every player should know.

Practice, practice, and practice them again and again. Once basic passing opportunities are learned, the players can have confidence that they can help produce a goal no matter what offensive play they are going into. The pass will go a long way toward setting up goals and scoring chances.

OFFENSIVE PLAYS

The main point of any offensive play is to draw the defenders away from the puck and puck carrier to create an "open man." The play, when executed correctly, allows one of the attackers to skate in alone, or at least significantly undeterred, without a defender threatening him. No play, regardless of its sophistication, can guarantee a goal. The offensive play is simply a formalized situation established by the attacking team to maximize the scoring chances. The play puts the correct offensive players in optimum positions on the ice to score a goal, while at the same time attempting to draw opposing players away from the play by putting them in the most restrictive or least opportunistic positions.

Every play must be practiced and executed consistently so every offensive player on the ice knows what the play is and how it is forming. I began to follow the precedent of a great idea set by a baseball Little League World Series coach a few years ago. This method is also used in basketball. This particular baseball coach would have his set offensive and defensive plays numbered and written down in a play book. Each player would memorize each play and its corresponding number. Then from the dugout, the coach would hold up big cards with large, thick numbers written on them corresponding to the play he wanted in that particular situation, so that all his players in the field could identify the play called for. There was no chance of confusion here; no excuses given, none accepted. The coach made the call and the players were expected to follow it. Some time later, while attending a college basketball game, I also noticed that the guard, as he moved the ball up the court, would call out different play numbers or offensive configurations to his teammates. Again, there was no confusion as to where each player should be and what his role was at that position.

Latching on to that play-calling proposition, I formulated the essential plays that the team employed regularly, wrote them down, assigned each play a number code and gave each player a play book. In practice, we worked on each play, how it was set up, and where each player should be at any given time within the play. Just to make sure, I worked each player both on the offense and defense through all the attack positions so every player would know where each of the others would be at any given time. When in a game and my team was beginning a rush up ice, I, or an assistant coach, would quickly survey the situation and shout out a play code to the team. In this manner there is no confusion as to which play to initiate, who will carry the puck, or where each player should be. As the players get older, I let them make their own decisions as to which play to initiate and call. When the youngest players play, that's a different story. Sometimes they get so excited that they even have the puck, they forget all offensive strategies and skate haphazardly up the ice with no set plan of action. By shouting out plays, it reminds all the players on the ice that they are there to participate as a team, and that with teamwork, they can make things happen.

In most plays, the puck carrier and leading and trailing players can easily be substituted or adapted to the immediate situation—depending on who has the puck and who needs it. Feel free to modify the plays as necessary to fit your particular situation. In addition, feel free to experiment with varying line and attack combinations to suit the play and talent of your particular team.

Following are several basic offensive plays that can be executed by any team, new or experienced, that will create the open man to produce the shot on goal.

The forwards approach the blue line staggered and spread across the ice. The right wing is leading and the left wing is trailing. The right wing carries the puck over the blue line and then drop passes left to the trailing center. The right wing breaks for the net outside of the defense, goes around back of the net and emerges on the left of the crease. In doing so, he pulls the right defense off

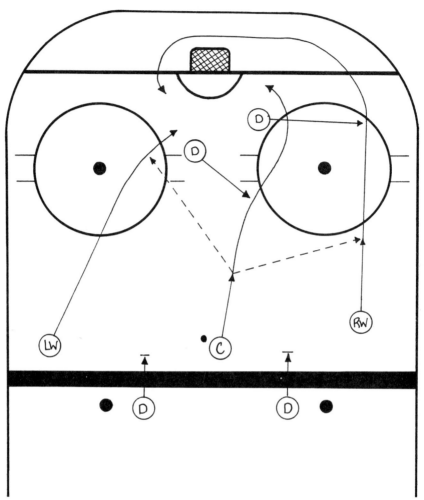

ILLUSTRATION 5-3. *A basic offensive give and go routine to start an attack.*

with him at least into the corner. The center, now with the puck, breaks directly toward the net slightly right, pulling the other defenseman toward him to the right. As the center approaches the face-off dots, he drop passes to the now trailing left wing and then heads for the front right side of the crease. The left wing heads toward the net slightly left and is clear to take the shot at will or pass to another forward.

The offensive line crosses the blue line with the left wing trailing slightly behind. The center is carrying the puck. As the lead wing and center cross the blue line together, the center breaks to

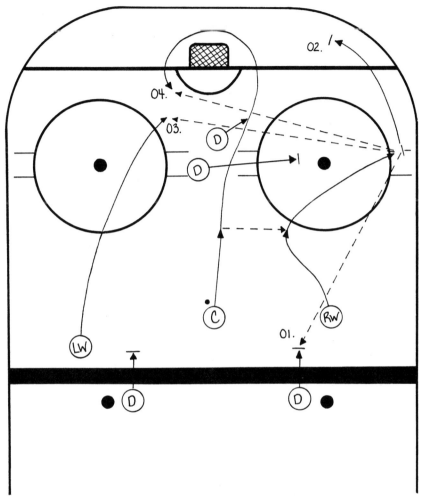

ILLUSTRATION 5-4. *Another basic play. The right wing carries deep into the zone and opens numerous passing opportunities to present scoring chances.*

ward the net with the lead wing breaking in toward the slot and then out to the boards. The center first passes the puck to the lead wing as he breaks to the boards, and then curls around back of the net to the edge of the crease opposite the now puckhandler and draws the defense with him. The puckhandler against the boards attempts to draw in the second defenseman across ice toward him. He then has the options to shoot the puck, pass to the center at the corner of the crease, pass back to either defensive player getting into position at the blue line, or preferably make a cross-ice pass to

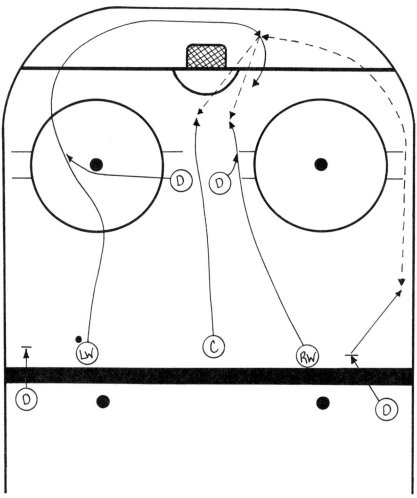

ILLUSTRATION 5-5. *The left wing carries deep and draws the defense in while the other forwards crash the net.*

the opposite wing, breaking in hard toward the net. After receiving the pass and shooting on goal, the wing then breaks toward the net for the potential rebound.

Again, as with most plays, the play can be reversed depending on which player is the puck carrier. The forward line crosses the blue line as a unit. As soon as they cross the blue line, the puck carrier, either of the wings, breaks out toward the boards and then around back of the net, drawing one of the defensemen with him. If the center is carrying the puck, he passes it over to one of the open wings to break. The center and right wing then break in close

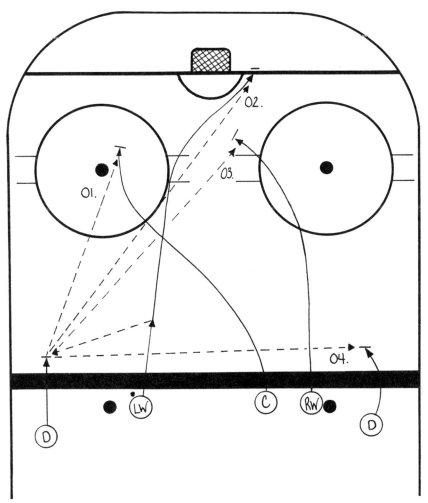

ILLUSTRATION 5-6. *A drop pass to the trailing defenseman is an ideal way to set up scoring opportunities. It allows the forwards time to maneuver into position in front of the net.*

together toward the net but not too tight together. The remaining defenseman can cover only one of the two approaching players. The puck carrier has the options of passing to either the crashing center or wing (whichever player is not covered) before he encircles the net or after he emerges from behind the net. The drop pass option to either trailing defenseman at the point is also open either before or after the puck carrier circles behind the net. The puck carrier can also attempt a stuff-in from the rear if all players appear covered. After the pass, the behind-the-net wing moves out to

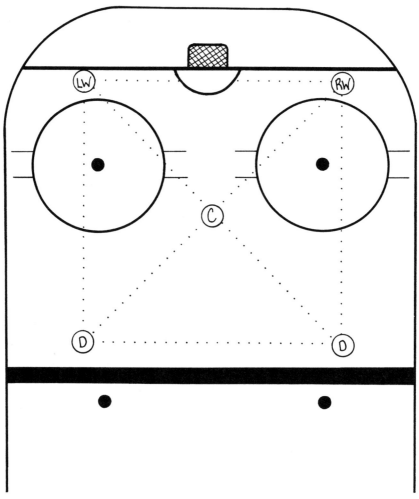

ILLUSTRATION 5-7. *The basic offensive "X" box is a good way to contain the puck in the zone while providing ample opportunities to move the puck to an open man.*

the opposite face-off dot and arcs back into his normal position ready for another pass to him or a rebound.

The forward line carries the puck as a unit across the blue line. A defenseman on the offensive team catches up to the play and trails closely behind the forwards. As this trailing defenseman crosses the blue line, the puck carrier drop passes the puck to the defenseman. The wing opposite the defenseman breaks toward the slot just in front of the net and the center breaks toward the face-off dot on the side of the ice that the puck is on. The wing who just dropped the puck to the defenseman breaks in toward the net, acts as a screen for the defenseman, then cuts and crosses the crease to the opposite side of the net at the corner. By now the other defenseman has joined the play inside the blue line. The defenseman currently holding the puck has significant options to pass to an open player, shoot for the net, or shoot for a deflection.

On a power play, the most basic offensive play is the "x-box" around the net, with a center pivot point in the slot. This is as basic an offensive setup as there is in hockey. It is also used as a basic offensive setup even without the man advantage. It essentially spreads all the offensive players in the offensive zone as far away from each other as possible to make it very difficult for a team with a man down to cover each player all the time. Four skaters cannot cover five skaters in all parts of the zone. An arrangement such as this one requires significant passing ability on the part of all of the players, as well as quick reflexes and a lot of patience.

The play is usually initiated with the puck being dumped in by the puck carrier from outside the red line either to the near or open corner with the puck being chased by one of the wings. If there are open lanes into the zone, the puck can be carried into the zone. Be careful not to go off-sides. It is very easy to get too anxious or overzealous and attempt to rush the puck into the zone, forcing an offside. In either event, the play starts with one of the wings in the corner controlling the puck until the remaining offensive players can get into position. Both wings take up residence alongside the boards somewhere between the face-off dots and the outside arc of the face-off circle. The center cruises the slot area between the face-off dots and up and down the ice from the crease to the top arcs of the face-off circles. The defensemen station themselves at the points, out from the boards about ten feet, just about five feet inside the blue line. This is the basic configuration for the offensive man-advantage attack. When you look down from above, it appears as an "X" on the ice with a center pivot point.

The team works the puck out away from the net along the boards and blue line, attempting to draw at least one and hopefully both defensemen or one of the remaining two forwards out of the defensive configuration toward the puckhandler. The offensive team is looking for the open man; that is, the man left uncovered by an opposing player. When or if this occurs, that means there is one offensive player who is probably double teamed and one or two offensive players who have no one near them. A pass is quickly sent over to either of these players for a shot in on goal.

This procedure may not always work to pull a man out from the play. It may then be necessary to work the puck in toward the goal. (See Illustration 5-8.) When this plan is initiated, the offensive

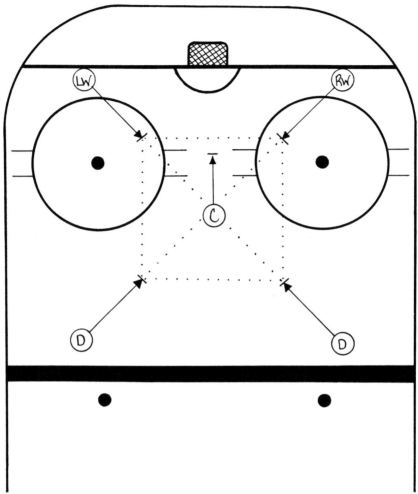

ILLUSTRATION 5-8. *By closing the "X" box tightly around the net, the goaltender has greater difficulty seeing the puck and there is a greater chance of a deflection.*

forward line and one defenseman begin to move the puck inward, closing the ranks in tighter around the net. The defensive players then have less room to maneuver and their ability to get to the puckhandler is greatly diminished. The goalie has less opportunity to see the puck as it is being passed through mazes of legs and sticks. A shot on goal has numerous chances for deflections and for a redirection. The idea here is again to find the open player. Sometimes, that open player may be the lone remaining defenseman at the point not squeezing in. It is an option to pass the puck back to the point for the one-timer or for redirection. The team can also pass back to the point to regroup if play is getting or disorganized or to force the defensive team to reorganize or scatter.

All man-advantage offensive plays evolve from this "X." Teams can easily improvise plays from the ice either in advance or as they are developing, following this lead. The keys to success in this formation are: to pass sharply; to spread out the attacking team; and to find the uncovered open player who has an opportunity for a shot to the goal. As with almost any formation, patience is important here. In a full two-minute man advantage, a team may only get two or three good shots on goal during the power play, but you only need one good shot to score. Toward the end of the penalty, a team may sometimes rush the shots or take shots that are neither practical nor feasible. The power play is disrupted and lost because the play is either broken up by the defensive team or botched by the offensive team. Teams can cut themselves out of at least fifteen seconds on each power play because of botched rush attempts. Excellent passing skills and patience are essential in this situation. It is a great idea to practice with the team spread out in this arrangement. Encourage players to pass to all corners of the zone and to all other players with quick, sharp, crisp passes. The quicker and crisper the passes, the less time and opportunity the defensive team has to get to the puck. Remember, it's a long way across the ice when only one man is covering the point. The puck covers the distance a lot quicker than a skater can.

Rotate the players around the box in the event that one player is caught out of position and needs to cover an off position. Prompt the players to pass using both regular and bounce passes off the side boards and end boards, and to practice passing around back of the net to the opposite wing using a "wrap-around" pass. Practice one-timers back to the point, with the defensemen alternating in to see which player has the best timing ability to make the play successful. Encourage your players to talk to each other out on the ice, to shout out directions and assistance, to give advice or suggestions. It may take some time before you find your number-one man-advantage line. The players who play together on the power play may not necessarily be the same players who play together on a regular shift at even strength. Your number-one power play unit will usually consist of three offensive forwards, one offensive defenseman and either one defensive scoring forward or one defensive defenseman. Experiment with different combinations of players at different positions. See which unit works best together. That unit will become your "bread and butter" line—the one line you can always count on to give you a top effort.

DEFENSIVE PLAYS

The main thoughts behind any defensive play are first to break up any scoring opportunities that the attacking team may be formulating, then to prevent any scoring chances from occurring, and finally to move the puck out of the zone.

Defensive Diamond Formation

There is one main defensive set-up that a team uses when at even strength. I call it the diamond formation because it resembles a baseball diamond. The diamond formation looks like this:

As the defense bases its strategy and reactions on what the offense is doing, a team cannot have distinctive and set defensive *plays*. A team can, however, have set defensive *strategies* that it can execute when under attack. In all of the strategies, the primary focus is to establish and control the zone. By establishing the zone, I mean that each defensive player must establish certain "territorial rights" to his portion of the ice. In addition, each defensive player must let the attacking players know that this ice is his to patrol and defend. The defense affirms this right to the ice by picking up the offensive player immediately he enters the zone or by clearing out his territory with forceful hitting and checking. Only when this "right to ice" is instituted can a team function effectively on defense.

As you can see in Illustration 5-9, the zones that are established by the defense are overlapping zones. There are no lines drawn on the ice or rules that say any one player covers only one rigidly defined area. The emphasis of teamwork is never so prevalent as it is in this defensive situation. The overlap of the defensive zones allows the defensive players bordering on either side of a zone to enter an adjacent area to provide assistance. This is frequently a necessity on defense as an offensive team will often attempt to "flood" a zone with two or three offensive players. Flooding a zone may cause inexperienced defensive players to panic and it may draw them out of their regular defensive positions to overprotect and crowd the flooded zone. When this occurs, the defense has left another zone empty. By flooding the zone and drawing away defensive players, the offense has hoped to leave an open offensive man in an opposite zone with a clear path to the goal. The puck is then directed to that open player for the scoring opportunity. For these reasons, players cannot randomly vacate their own zones.

It is also important to stress to the defensive team that the players are not permitted to scramble all over the ice into each other's areas at will to retrieve the puck. Discipline is a key element in the defensive zone. I have found that throughout junior hockey,

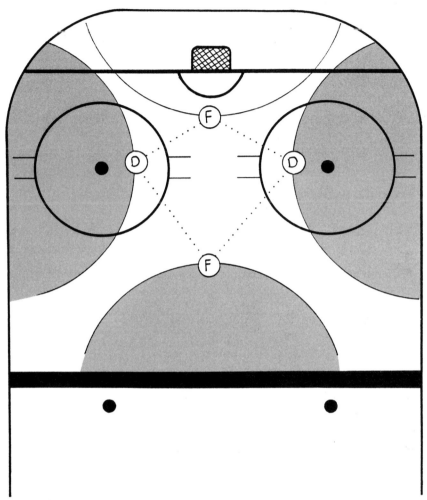

ILLUSTRATION 5-9. *Basic defensive zone coverage areas. The shaded areas are the prime responsibility of the named player; the white areas are overlapping zones with multiple coverage.*

the success of an offensive attack is attributed not necessarily to the determination or skill of the offensive team as it is to the lack of discipline on behalf of the defensive team. In a scrambling free-for-all situation, most of the younger players will panic, and some will want to be heroes. As a result, the entire defensive team on the ice heads toward the puck (and I've even had the goalie skate toward the puck as well), leaving the defense in shambles. The key to organized defense is discipline. Encourage, stimulate, persuade, sanction—do anything you can to get your defensive team players

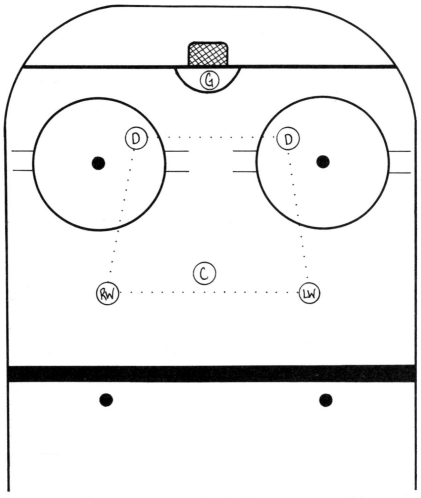

ILLUSTRATION 5-10. *A basic defensive box set up around the net to protect the zone. The center acts as a free floating forward to chase the puck.*

to stay in their zones. The diamond, when played correctly, has proven to be a highly effective weapon against the offense. Although it is not impenetrable, it is the number one line of defense against an offensive attack.

Defensive Box Formation

The defensive box is used concurrently with the defensive diamond. Each team should be able to move swiftly and decisively into the defensive box. This box is used primarily in short-handed

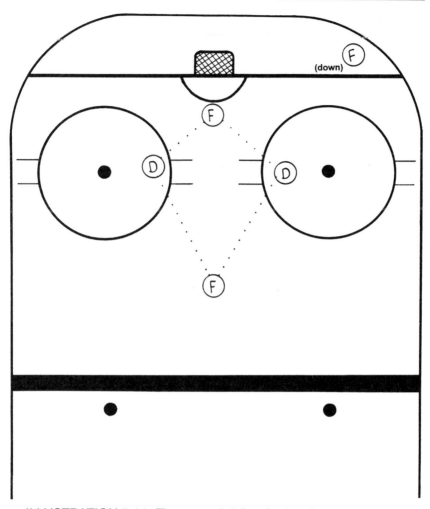

ILLUSTRATION 5-11. *The rotated defensive box is put into action when one of the forwards or defensemen is taken out of play.*

situations when a team is killing a penalty. It may also be used when a team finds itself one man down due to either a fallen player on the ice, a player who has lost his stick, or an injured player who has not yet been spotted by the referees. The defensive box is played nearly identically on the ice as the diamond, but with one fewer player. The zones are obviously larger, resulting in one player being required to cover a greater area. You can still allow for some zone overlap between adjacent areas, but the players must be more disciplined and selective in their player assignments and action choices as they enter an adjoining zone. The overlap of the zones

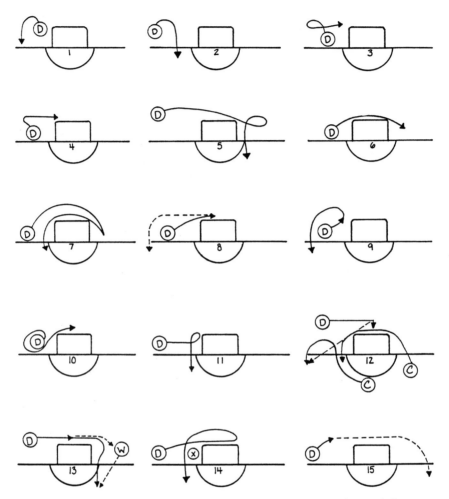

ILLUSTRATION 5-12. *Fifteen basic escape maneuvers that a defense-man may use when carrying the puck deep into the defensive zone.*

becomes significantly smaller, maybe for just a few feet depending on the skills of the individual players.

When in the defensive box, the primary objective is to clear the offensive zone of the puck by any legal means. This can be accomplished by the defensive team stripping players of the puck via poke checks, stick checks, and body checks. In addition, the defensive players should retrieve loose pucks that the offense has lost. When the puck is claimed by a defensive player, the defense as a unit must decide whether to shoot the puck out in a dump or skate and carry the puck out of the zone to start the offense. I always tell my players, "When in doubt, dump it out!" and when I say "dump," I mean high above the heads of all the players where no one can get it, so, "Ice it!"

Rotated Box

There is a slight variation to the box, and I call it the rotated box. It resembles a playing card diamond. In the rotated box, there is a point man who guards between the two offensive points at the blue line. Another player stands in front of the net low in the slot to clear out the crease of attackers. The remaining two players patrol the two wing lanes up and down the ice. Using this rotated box can often momentarily confuse the offense, as well as provide a cut-off for cross-ice and long down-ice passes that the offense attempts. Although opponents can often quickly adapt their play to the rotated box by rotating their offense to fill in the gaps, by the defense shifting back and forth between the regular box and the rotated box, it can keep the offense guessing, moving, and hopefully unstructured. It might even be enough to shut down the attack at a critical time.

Your number one defensive penalty killing unit will usually consist of two defensive players; one defensive forward and an excellent face-off man, probably a center. Control of the puck is essential in penalty killing. If your team can control the puck for even a few seconds longer in your own zone, then that's a few seconds less that the attacking team has the puck. A "won" face-off can give you that advantage—control of the puck for a dump or carry-out.

There will be times, however, that a dump-out is not practical, necessary, or prudent. Once control of the puck is established by the defensive team in its own zone and the attacking team is giving up the attack or is not pursuing the puck for whatever reason (like a line change), the correct play in most situations is to carry the puck out of the zone. By carrying the puck out instead of dumping it out, the team has the opportunity to establish an offensive attack strategy. You can't constantly dump the puck out or you'll never have any offense. I have illustrated here twenty-one defensive skating maneuvers that a player carrying the puck can initiate in order to get the puck out of the zone safely, fifteen plays from deep in the zone on the goal line and six plays from near the blue line or in the neutral zone.

The fifteen skating maneuvers from the end boards are:

1. Direct to boards
2. Direct up center
3. Boards to off-wing
4. Fake to on-wing

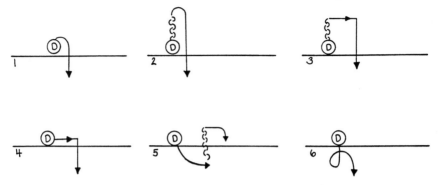

ILLUSTRATION 5-13. *Six defensive maneuvers a defenseman may use when carrying the puck near the defensive blue line.*

   5. Escape off-wing
   6. Off-wing
   7. Counter
   8. Reverse pass
   9. Fake off-wing
  10. 360 degrees
  11. Escape on-wing
  12. Stop—center pick
  13. Give and go
  14. Counter and escape
  15. Ring around

The six skating maneuvers from near the blue line or in the neutral zone are:

   1. Tight control turn
   2. Backward, tight turn, forward
   3. Backward, stop, forward
   4. Step out
   5. Forward, step out, backward
   6. 360 degrees

If players on the team understand what a defenseman might do with the puck, they can begin to maneuver themselves into position to either assist the defenseman as he escapes with the puck or be in a position to accept the pass from the defenseman to start the offense.

Every player should also remember the following: When caught deep in the zone with the puck with opposing players either attacking or defending against the rush out, the best defensive clearing maneuver is always to clear the puck to the corners and set up the zone clearing pass from there. Never attempt to clear the zone by shooting the puck up ice through the middle of the zone. If each player on the team remembers and follows these two simple suggestions, then each will always know where to put the puck in case he panics and where to get the puck if he wants to carry it out of the zone.

With sound defensive hockey, every team should be able to at least stand its ground against a superior team. It doesn't matter if your team scores fifty goals in a game. If you give up fifty-one goals, you still lose. Conversely, you can win with just one goal if your team keeps the opposing team's score to zero.

Practice good, sound fundamentals. Only with a clear understanding and mastery of the basic hockey skills can a player or team begin to initiate and exhibit the fancy maneuvers and skill competence that turns the average player into a great player and the average team into a championship team.

Now your team has a set of plays to practice and learn. Play books are stuffed deep into the pockets and probably even school folders of every player on the team. But there still remain two players on the team who read and memorize the material but know that, except for some very small parts, very little of it applies to them. They are the goalies. They don't carry the puck across the blue line, they don't fore-check, they can't back-check. Just what do they do? Well, netminders are a whole different matter. They are a breed apart—so let's take a closer look at them and their role on the team in the next chapter.

6.

GOALTENDERS—
A BREED APART

"Mom! Mom! Guess what! I signed up for the hockey team!"

"Wow, you did? Fantastic! The hockey team, huh? Well, I'm ... I'm proud of you, dear! I like to see you join things. But honey, I didn't know that you could skate that well."

"I can't, so I signed up as a goalie."

"Oh ... oh ... really? A goalie ... um ... that's great. Oh, by the way sweetheart, ... just out of curiosity, ... why on earth be a goalie?"

WHY ON EARTH BE A GOALIE?

Why would anyone in their right mind want to become a goaltender? What would cause a perfectly sound human being to place himself in front of rock-hard vulcanized pieces of rubber fired directly at him at sometimes over one hundred miles an hour? Why would anyone want to put himself through this type of torture? I cannot speak for anyone else, but I can only guess that others feel as I do; the goalie is the center of attention. You can play a game without a defenseman or a wing, but you really can't play without a goalie. The play and the action revolve around putting the puck in the net, and the goalie is in the center of that net. The goalie is constantly involved in the action, always on the ready, always eager to play. They don't sit down on the bench for a rest, they don't take shifts, they don't escape to adjust their equipment in the locker room between shifts. The goalie is an integral part of the game, and every one of them knows it.

The goaltender's primary responsibility is to stop the puck. It is not to clear the zone, initiate play, be a cheerleader, or score goals. It is the goaltender's job, above and beyond everything else, to prevent the puck from going into the net. The art (and it is an art) of stopping a puck is accomplished by a combination of lightning quick reflexes, tremendous skill, knowledge of the physics of the game, and a lot of luck. Any goalie who tells you otherwise has yet to understand how to play the position. There is not now nor has there ever been a goalie who can do it all just on skill. There is so much involved in playing the position that one human being cannot possibly be so skillful while wearing all that equipment that he can say there is no element other than skill involved in the making of a great goalie.

The goaltender is an essential part of the game. The game revolves around him and will either stop or continue based on his decisions. The action moves quickly or slowly depending on how the goalie handles the puck. The play at times is totally dependent on the goalie. Besides the fact that the goalie is the last hope to stop the puck, it is often the goalie who initiates the offensive attack by setting up the puck for the defenseman. It is the goalie who is the star of the defense. There is never a dull moment in the crease. Even when the puck is at the other end of the rink, the goalie must be mentally involved in the play. The puck can travel the entire length of the ice in just a few short seconds. The goalie must be on top of the play at all times.

When the game is over, more often than not the fans leave the arena saying either the goalie was hot and really shut down the offense, or the goalie was awful and really let up some poor goals. If any other player on the team makes a mistake during the game, there are plenty of other players on the ice who can cover for him. In fact, even a player on the other team can unwittingly cover mistakes of a player and many of the fans will never know it. But let the goalie make just one single stupid mistake, and the whole rink knows immediately because there is a big red light flashing behind him to announce it to the world. But in spite of all its drawbacks and pitfalls, there is no other position in sports like it. Neither is there a type of player like the goalie.

WHO CAN BE A GOALIE?

I believe goalies are born and not created. There are certain personality traits that must come out during a game that are difficult to learn. The quickness of mind and body and the aggressiveness necessary to make a good goalie often come more easily to some children than others. You often read how goaltenders need a certain type of personality, a certain demeanor, a certain disposition that allows them to take wins and losses all in stride. But what about talent? What kind of athletic ability does a child need in order to become an effective goaltender?

Skating Skill

Regardless of what the young player who opened this chapter thinks, the goalie needs to be an excellent skater. In fact, a goalie needs to be one of the better skaters on the team. Goalies are constantly up and down, skating side to side and back and forth, instantly (and literally) standing on their heads at times. The netminder needs good, stable feet and strong legs to keep him going all game. Remember, the goalie doesn't get a change of shift; he's in the net for the entire game. A goaltender needs the physical and mental stamina to be able to stay in the game.

Physical Strength

Remember that goalies carry a lot of equipment, sometimes an extra forty pounds as they get in more advanced leagues. After a game, that same forty pounds can weigh fifty to sixty pounds with perspiration. In addition, goalies place themselves in positions to be roughed up by the opposing team. When you see a pile of players in front of the net after a stoppage of play, the goaltender is usually at the bottom of it all. When a goaltender goes around back of the net to stop a wrap-around pass, he is often blind-sided by an attacking player and takes the direct hit. Often, the goaltender is pushed, shoved, and checked back into the upright or cross bar of the net. That bar is made of hardened steel, three inches in diameter. A goalie needs to be able to take a lot of physical punishment in the course of a game.

Reflexes

Lightning quick reflexes, although a nice talent to have, are not necessary and usually not present when starting out as a child. Most of the youngsters who play mite hockey haven't got lightning quick shots anyway. As a goaltender matures and grows both physically and mentally, his reflexes sharpen as well. Regular practice in the crease helps sharpen those reflexes.

Mental Strength

In addition to having a good basic skill level and a desire to mind the net, a goalie also needs to be a smart player. He needs to be able to analyze different situations quickly and plan and act according to these analyses. A good goalie must be able to study the game and the mechanics of the game and apply that knowledge to his position. He needs to know how to play the angles, the rebounds, and the percentages. He needs to be able to calculate angles of deflection and shot angle instantly and to react accordingly. Like reflexes, these skills are sharpened over time, but a modicum of skills needs to be present from the outset.

A goaltender needs a level and stable personality. He needs to be very patient above all. He cannot be too aggressive, anxious, or hasty. He needs to know how to "sit the position" and make the play and players come to him. He needs to know when to let the other players make the first move, as then and only then, can he react to the move. Again, these talents will develop over time, but they need to be present as seeds to begin with.

Some coaches think that anticipation is a key element of being a goaltender. I disagree. Anticipation is just any player's ability to guess what might happen in any given situation. If the game of hockey is a game with repetitive actions and reactions, then anticipation may be beneficial. But as we all know, it's not! In hockey, there is no starting gun and no race to win. Shooters sometimes don't even know what they themselves will do next with the puck, so why should a goalie attempt to guess. A goaltender needs to be able to read the angles of deflection so that he can prepare to block shots coming in on goal. He can benefit from mental agility and anticipation, as long as his body doesn't move before the shot is released. Anticipation can get goalies into a lot of trouble, and allow them to leave the goal vulnerable when they should be patiently waiting for the shooter to give up the puck.

Courage

Finally, a goalie needs to be courageous. It takes a lot of—I'm not quite sure what—to stand up only yards in front of an oncoming hard puck and purposefully fling your body in front of it to stop it. The most important thing a goalie needs to realize is that, except for a few instances, the puck won't really hurt. Once the goalie stands up to the shot and takes it in the pads or blocker or some place where it won't hurt, he will realize that even the hard shots don't hurt. This knowledge minimizes the mental advantage of the hard shot. The goaltender wears enough protective padding made of space age material and plastics that regardless of how hard and fast the puck travels, it won't do any real damage.

While a direct slapshot to the face mask will sting a lot and ring some bells, the child who is wearing the proper equipment properly fitted will not suffer any damage to his face or mask. Of course, this shot is scary and may leave the goalie a little "gun shy," but that's understandable. As a coach, I never force any player back into a game if he doesn't want to be in. If a player needs time to recover, that's all right by me. While it is not my preference, I would choose to play the game without a goaltender rather than force a child to play who didn't want to play. I don't follow the "get right back on your horse" theory. A child will decide for himself when to play again, and when the "hockey bug" bites hard enough, he'll play.

Concentration

Finally, I believe that to be a good goalie, a child needs excellent concentration. The goalie is out on the ice for the entire game. It is very easy to become distracted and lose concentration. Just one moment of relaxed attention can lead to a mistake and ultimately a lost goal—or worse, an injury. Concentration is something that cannot be taught. I find that although it is possible to sharpen or hone concentration, it just cannot be taught. Unlike many previous skills which can be learned over time, the ability to concentrate on the play of the game must be present to some degree from the beginning.

If your child comes to you and tells you he just signed up to be a goalie, don't panic, don't fret, don't worry. Instead be glad that he chose a position of leadership, responsibility, and skill that will not only help him become a better player and overall athlete, but a better individual as well. Oh, and do start saving money.

BASIC SKILLS AND PROCEDURES

Stance and Equipment

The basic stance or starting position for all goalies is the goalie crouch. The goalie crouch is a highly specialized position that puts the goalie on the balls of his feet to move to stop the puck with ease and agility. Begin by bending the knees slightly. Leg pads should be together straight up and down or with only a very slight split between them. Some goalies will spread their legs too much and bend the knees inward sharply at the top. This method is not recommended as it leaves what is known as the "five hole," a gaping space just between the legs above the stick and below the knees. With the pads together, there is a barrier of leg pad that is impenetrable. The upper body is bent forward slightly at the waist. The back is held straight, not curved down. The head is tilted upward to see the play, but not straining. If the goalie finds that his neck is stretched too much and is causing a cramp at the back of the neck, then he should not bend as much at the waist.

The catching glove is held open facing the play. It is held out about six inches from the side of the body between the lower hip and the knee area. The wrist is stiff enough to hold the glove steady but flexible enough to be moved quickly side to side. The glove is tilted slightly outward and up with the catching pocket held at about the three o'clock position. This puts the glove in the optimum position to catch pucks that come in high, low, or out away from the body. The elbow is bent slightly toward the back and is used as a pivot point against the body to raise or lower the glove.

The stick mitt is (obviously) on the hand that is holding the stick. The bottom of the stick blade is flat against the ice surface. The blocker is held out from the side of the body a few inches, not flat against the pants or jersey. When held properly in the goalie crouch, the top portions of the flat surfaces of the stick will be slightly tilted toward the play with the butt end of the stick slightly out. This is to prevent any unusual rebounds or caroms directly off the stick. Incoming pucks can hit any portion of the stick and deflect down to the ice in front of the goalie. The blocker will also be slightly tilted toward the ice to minimize rebounds, but it can easily be rotated around a vertical axis to any position to create any angle of deflection.

The stick blade should be out from the skates several inches. It should not be held flat and stiffly against the toes of the skates. If it is held flat and hard against the skates, a puck hit hard against the stick will rebound directly back to the shooter. If held out from the toes, a hard hit shot will hit the blade, push the blade back, and be cushioned by the stick and arm holding it. There will not be a rebound.

Remember, the netminder should be on the balls of his feet. This allows quick and complete movement in any direction. On the ice, the skates are positioned with the toes just out on the red line of the crease. The body should be square, facing the play. If a face-off is being held in one of the near circles, the goalie should position himself on the red-line corners of the crease directly between the face-off dot and the net. He should not be afraid to look back over his shoulder to see where the net is located in relation to himself and the face-off dot. While in a crouch facing the play awaiting the drop of the puck, the goalie can use the shaft of the stick and tap backward against the upright bars of the net to check location and position in the crease. (See photo on page 133.)

Bad Habits

As a player matures and gains more experience in the goal, he will begin to adjust and adapt his skills to his particular likes and dislikes. As long as this adaptation is in the direction of improvement, it is a good thing. It is important, however, that coaches help pre-

The goalie is down in his basic crouch. He is actually a little too bent, but the idea is right. He is ready to stop anything.

vent bad habits at an early stage. Try not to let your goaltenders assume bad stances and get "lazy" in their crouch. Look for warning signs that your goalie is getting tired, lazy, or sloppy. Usually, the player begins to let the glove just hang down at his side with no upward extension. He may begin to sit back on his haunches or sink too deep in his crouch. Watch for specifics such as:

- ☐ The stick pulled way back and the butt end pulled down and back instead of held straight up and out.

- ☐ The goalie's elbow resting on top of the leg pad. This causes a gap to open between the ice and the bottom of the blade near the toe of the stick.

- ☐ The blocker mitt held tight against the body resting on the hip.

- ☐ The leg pads split with the feet wide apart and the knees resting against themselves inwardly.

- ☐ The head held down and the goalie using his eyes to look up at the play.

These are all bad habits that can quickly develop in a goalie. If your goalie exhibits these signs at the beginning of practice, either he has developed habits that need to be changed or he is possibly too weak physically to play the position.

They are also signs that a goalie is getting tired or weak. If you see these signs developing toward the end of practice or a game, then the goalie may be short on stamina. Help construct some exercises that will strengthen the necessary muscles to prevent this from happening. These exercises need not be anything more than a few minutes extra in the goal for each practice. One of my favorite exercises is to have the goalie wear all his equipment around the house on days without games. Just wearing the heavy pads helps build up stamina and tolerance of the weight and feel of the equipment, as well as assist the youngster in developing balance and maneuverability while wearing the pads.

BASIC POSITIONING

In assuming the basic stance or crouch of the goalie, the netminder is putting himself in the optimum position to block most incoming shots. The arms, legs, and head are all placed in positions from which it is easiest and fastest to move in any direction. To further help the goaltender, positioning on the ice is equally important. The goalie uses the crease lines on the ice to position himself directly in front of the play. This alone, however, is not sufficient to stop a goal. By moving out from the goal mouth to the top or the edge of the crease or even beyond, the goalie is "cutting down the angle." Cutting down the angle is used most often on breakaways or on open shots from the tops of the circles.

What this essentially means is that the player is presenting the oncoming attacker with less of a line of sight of the net at which to shoot. (See the photo on page 135.) The further the goalie comes out of the net, the less net there is for the attacker to see. Of course, that also means that the further the goaltender comes out of the crease, the more likely it is that the attacker can maneuver himself around him toward the open net. Even though the goaltender is an excellent skater, his pads will prevent him from having the maneuverability and agility of a forward. It will be nearly impossible for the netminder to stretch and contort his body in a way that will prevent a goal in this situation. This is one of those cases when he needs to rely on sheer luck.

Each individual goaltender is faced with the task of finding the line on the ice which he cannot cross. This line is an imaginary line beyond which he will be unable to continue. He will be able to come out of the crease to this line, but not beyond. The line will vary for every goalie. Its location will depend on a number of factors which include: the agility and skill of the individual; the physi-

The goalie is slightly out to cut down the angle. By coming out of the crease, he decreases the amount of net available to the shooter's sight or aim.

cal height and arm length of the goalkeeper; and the quickness of his reflexes in reacting to a situation. A goalie knows that up to this line, he is physically able to stop most shots and handle most dekes. Past this line, there will be little chance to stop either the shooter or the puck.

These examples are demonstrated more clearly in the photos on page 136. As the forward makes a move around the goalie for the goal, the netminder will move laterally with the player and puck. The timing of the move will be critical and reflexes will be tested, as the goalie needs to keep himself between the puck and the net at all times. At some point the goalie will need to stretch out toward the puck or across the goal mouth. Here physical height and arm length, or at least the ability to make himself "big," is important. If the previous two attributes do the job and prevent the attacker from scoring, then the physical ability of the netminder should kick in next as he needs to recover quickly back to his skates and reposition himself in the crease for the potential rebound.

BASIC SAVES

There are several types of saves that a goaltender can employ to stop the puck. Each save is distinct in its movements and each

Sometimes the goalie needs to come far out of the net to cut down the angle.

This goalie has done a nice job of coming out of the net, making himself "big," and plugging all the holes. The puck actually skidded wide.

has distinct situations calling for its use. Every goaltender should be able to properly execute any of the saves for any scoring chance. The different types of saves are the glove save, stick save, blocker save, leg pad save, kick save, toe save, skate save, and body save.

Glove Save

The glove save is the most basic save that a goaltender employs. Nearly every child in North America has caught a ball with a baseball glove at one time or another. The glove save is essentially the same. The netminder moves his arm on a pivot at the shoulder and also moves his hand on a pivot at the wrist to change the angle of the glove face and pocket to meet any incoming shot. The shot does not necessarily have to be on the "glove side" of the goaltender. The glove may be used wherever the hand can reach the puck.

The glove save is also the safest save a goalie can make. In a glove save, the netminder has total control of the puck. It is easiest to drop the puck off for a teammate or freeze it for a stoppage of play when in control of the puck.

Traditionally, goaltenders have "good glove hands." That is, the gloved hand is usually the quickest and most versatile part of the body used to stop a shot. Shooters will often shy away from shooting to the glove side of the goalie. But a goalie cannot stop a shot he cannot reach. For that reason, shooters will often force a goalie down to the ice with a deke or fake around, and then when the goalie is down or going down, will shoot high to the glove side where the goalie cannot snare it. Another shooter's trick is to deke the goalie to the right side, and when the goalie is pulled right, toward the feign, shoot to the left glove side where the netminder can't reach it.

The glove save is one of the goalie's primary defenses. That is why it is stressed never to commit yourself in a breakaway. The quick glove used properly can cover almost half the net. (See photo on page 138.)

Stick Save

When the stick is held at the optimum angle and at the proper location on the shaft—just as the shaft and blade intersect—the stick is perfectly balanced on the pivot point of the wrist. If the netminder is having difficulty controlling the stick from this hold, more than likely the stick is either too long or too heavy for the player. When using the stick to stop the puck, there are two types of stops that are used. The goaltender can either stop the shot with a cushioning drop stop or a directed rebound stop.

*Glove save! The glove rises up to snare the puck with no rebound.
Notice the goalie keeps his eyes on the puck all the way
into the glove.*

CUSHIONING DROP STOP

In the cushioning drop stop, the goaltender holds the stick softly in the hand with the thumb behind the blade, with the blade perpendicular to the incoming shot. At the moment—or just before—the puck hits the stick, the goalie tilts the stick blade downward toward the ice slightly. When the puck hits the stick on any part, it will drop and fall immediately to the ice directly in front of the goaltender. This save is used to control rebounds when there aren't any attackers approaching the net. It gives the goalie complete control of the puck.

DIRECTED REBOUND STOP

In the directed rebound stop, the stick is held stiffly in the hand against the toes of the skates. As the puck is approaching, the goalie decides in which direction he wants the rebound to go. The goalie rotates the stick blade toward the intended direction of rebound. As the puck hits the blade of the stick, because it is held firmly and does not "give," the puck is met with an equal and resistant opposing force and will rebound sharply off in the direction the stick is angled toward. This save is used to clear pucks into the corners or to the side boards quickly when an attacker is rapidly approaching behind the shot looking for a rebound. With lots of practice, a goaltender can also learn to steer rebounds directly toward a teammate for immediate control. (See photo on page 140.)

Blocker Save

The blocker is also known as the stick mitt or the waffle. The saves that the goalie makes with the blocker mitt are very similar to those made by the stick. The most common save is the directed rebound save. By tilting the blocker pad slightly in any direction, the netminder can direct the rebound of the puck toward any section of the ice or toward any player. Stoppage by the blocker is very easily accomplished. Next to the leg pads, the blocker is the piece of equipment with the largest area. The goalie just needs to meet the puck with the blocker. The puck hits the mitt and drops to the ice. In addition, by moving the blocker mitt toward the shot as it approaches and meeting the shot with "force," the netminder can rebound the puck a significant distance with considerable accuracy.

Because of the severe physical restrictions caused by the arm pads, the goaltender gets a lot of work on the stick side during a game. Many attackers know that the weight of the stick plus the weight of the blocker plus somewhat limited arm movement will provide for goals when the shot is high to the stick side. This is probably any goaltender's most vulnerable area. Unlike the glove that can get high to the corners with a long arm, it is very difficult to reach the upper corner to protect it with the blocker, especially when the goalie is down on the ice with the stick arm bent down to keep the stick low.

A common and serious problem to avoid when stopping the puck with the blocker is a tendency to twist the blocker arm open so the glove or back portion of the mitt is facing the shot. Some young goaltenders will move their hands up and away from the body while twisting the mitt so the hand is exposed to the puck instead of keeping the flat blocker portion toward the puck. When a goalie twists his hand and arm open, it exposes the fingers and palm to the shot. If the puck hits the hand, the knuckles and fingers are trapped against the shaft of the stick and can easily be fractured. This is one common problem to correct early on when training new goaltenders.

Leg Pad Save

The two leg pads are the largest pieces of equipment that the goalie wears. They are also by far the heaviest, the most padded, and the most likely to be used to stop pucks. It is estimated that

The goaltender's stick is a very versatile defensive weapon. Not only can it be used to stop shots, here it is used to poke check a puck away from danger.

the goaltender uses the leg pads to stop almost eighty percent of the shots on goal in a game. If given a choice, the goaltender would prefer to stop as many shots as possible with the glove. The goalie has the best control of the puck when it is caught, but goaltenders often are not given the choice as an opponent will often fire the puck into the goalie's leg pads. With the introduction of new, lighter synthetic materials, the weight of the pads has been reduced significantly. These pads are, however, still of considerable weight and size especially for the youngest, smallest players. It is extremely difficult to raise the pads high off the ice to stop a shot. At most, a few inches to nine inches high is about all that most goalies will be able to raise the pads.

Although the primary duty and responsibility of the leg pads is to stop incoming low and hard shots, they can also be used, to a significantly lesser degree, to direct rebounds. As the puck hits the soft, cushioning material, it drops to the ice at the goalie's feet to be easily controlled by him or a teammate. Most importantly, the puck has been stopped.

Due to their size, the pads take up a significant portion of the mouth of the goal. Fortunately for goalies, many shooters lacking finesse or skill will simply hit the pads even if the goaltender never moves them. The problem arises when the goaltender moves about in the crease, creating openings on either side of the pads or between the legs. This is, of course, a hazard of the profession. A goalie can't just stand, he must move.

The key lies then in *how* to move. The secret is to keep the protective, flat outer face of the pads toward the shooters as much as possible. In this position, the pad is widest and the leg is least exposed. The goalie should move across the crease laterally (sideways) in a gliding or sliding motion. By sliding across the crease laterally, the pads remain closer together, the gap is significantly smaller, and the body remains square to the play.

The side slide is accomplished first by *not* having sharp skate blades. The goalie needs a dulled blade or else the skate will shave too deeply into the ice and stop in mid-slide. (In this example, we'll say the goalie is moving from his right to his left across the crease.) Second, the goalie turns the toe of the left skate out a few inches in the direction of travel. Next, he pushes off with the side and heel of the blade of the right skate. Once the body is in motion, the goaltender pushes the left heel back out toward the center line to straighten out the left skate and pad to square it back to the play. The momentum of the body in motion will cause the goalie to move across the crease to the opposite upright of the net, bringing the right leg and skate with him. The movement is completed with the body sliding sideways across the crease.

The speed of travel and how quick the slide is completed will depend on how hard the netminder pushes off with the opposite skate. The harder the push, the faster he will move. Of course, the goalie must practice sliding across the crease to each opposite upright goal post. It is good practice to alternate sliding back and forth across the crease until it becomes second nature. This is another area where it is important to practice enough that both legs are equally strong and there is no dominant side and weaker side.

By using this sliding method of moving about, the goalie keeps the pads squarely facing the play with little gap between. By keeping the pads square, there is the greatest chance that the puck will hit the pads for the save.

Kick Save

The kick save is similar in use to the pad save but with a significant variation. In the pad save, the netminder keeps the pads still and straight; in the kick save, the goalie actually kicks out one of the leg pads to meet the approaching puck and redirects the puck out away from the goal. Because of the length of the goalie's legs and their low position along the ice, this type of save is usually employed when a puck is headed to the lower corners of the net. Because of the difficulty of getting the pad flush against the ice, the save is used when the puck is traveling from about eight inches to eighteen inches off the ice surface. Because this is a very committed save from which it is very difficult to recover, the goalie must be certain beyond any doubt that this is the only save to use.

To perform the kick save, the goalie must first determine: that the incoming puck is the correct height above the ice; that he would have significant difficulty reaching the puck with either the catching glove, the stick mitt, or the stick; and that the puck would not hit the leg pads unless they were moved into it. All of these decisions must be made in an instant, and they are often made reflexively.

If the puck is approaching the goal on the goaltender's lower left side, and he has decided to stop the puck with the kick save, he will raise to the ball and toes of his right foot. In the raise, the goalie slightly rotates his body toward the left and begins to kick out the left leg pad. The momentum and force of the kick will bring the leg and rest of the body along with it and the body will complete the rotation toward the left. The pad does not travel along the surface of the ice; the skate is not contacting the ice.

The idea is to get the pad to its proper location and to meet the puck in the crease as soon as possible with as little interference or friction as possible while the skate and pad are still in the air traveling toward the corner of the net. If the skate blade is traveling along the ice surface, friction slows down the movement. In addition, there is the possibility of jamming the heel of the skate into the ice when the skate is tilted up and it may stick. Unlike a blocker stop where the goalie sometimes has time to adjust and align the position of the mitt, the kick save is performed in one fluid movement. Timing is crucial. The goalie needs to meet the puck with the leg pad as it is entering the crease. The goalie cannot kick out the leg and wait for the puck to arrive; the puck and the pad must arrive at the impact point at the same time.

The kick save is often a "last resort" save because of the difficulty the goaltender has in recovering. It is an awkward save from which to return quickly to the ready crouch position. The kick save is often referred to as "the splits" because of the way the legs are split wide open. Recover from the kick save back to the ready stance as quickly as possible and in any way possible. The goalie should never turn his back to the play; he should keep watching it at all times.

By using the kick save, because of momentum of the pad moving at a contrasting angle to the line of flight of the puck, the puck will also be redirected away from the goal. The kick save is an excellent way to break up attacks and to get the puck out of trouble to a teammate for zone clearance.

Toe Save

The toe save is a variation of the kick save. The pad is not flung out toward the puck, but is stretched out quickly toward the approaching puck. Unlike the kick save, the weight of the skate and leg are resting on the pad and the pad side is slid flat along the ice into position with the pad front facing the shot. The skate boot is stretched and tilted slightly so the toe is pointing out prominently beyond the pad. The idea here is that the pointing of the toe will fill the small gap left open just in the corner where the goal post and the ice meet. Keep the face of the pad toward the puck. The pad surface is used as further protection and stopping area.

The toe save is usually initiated from a kneeling position. Unlike the kick save in which the goaltender is standing and will fall to the ice on the kick, the goalie may already be on the ice and so will have much greater control of the leg and pad. Placement of the toe will be easier, but most certainly should be just as quick. If the netminder is standing, it is best to fall to one knee to initiate the toe save. (See photo on page 144.)

Because the toe will be pointing out toward the corners of the net, the leg pad itself will be flat side out exposed to the play. The netminder will have maximum coverage at the sides of the goal mouth. A significant disadvantage to this type of save, however, is that as the goalie extends his leg to a corner, he leaves a wide, gaping hole between the legs through which the puck can be redirected. Unlike the kick save where the goalie falls flat to the ice and the hole is quickly covered, the toe save leaves the hole exposed the entire time the goalie is down on the ice. The best defense against this opening is for the goalie to bring the stick mitt and blocker board down to the ice with the edge of the long, vertical side of the stick blade flush against the ice surface in front of the hole. This covers the hole until the goalie can recover back to the ready stance. (See photo on page 144.)

On some occasions, the goalie, while already down having just performed a toe save on one side, will be forced to make another toe save on the opposite side. Unlike with the kick save or the splits, this is easily accomplished. The goalie will already be on his knees; it is just as easy to slide out the other leg pad to the opposite corner. This is known as going down into the "butterfly flop." A goalie who performs this maneuver a lot and who prefers to go down to the ice rather than stand up and watch and react to the play is called a "butterfly" type of goalie. These goalies claim that by getting close to the ice, they can better see the play and the ice

The goalie has just stopped the puck with the blocker and is directing the rebound away from the waiting attacker.

Stretching the pad way out to make the save is routine for this goalie. The pads will be used to stop most of the shots on goal.

surface through the legs and sticks of the players and are better prepared to stop the puck. (See photo on page 146.)

Skate Save

The skate save is made with the blade of the skate, not with the boot of the skate. Of course, there will be times when the goalie doesn't have the option of where to stop a puck and that's why the boot of the skate is encased in hard-shell plastic. The plastic helps prevent injuries to the foot and ankle bones.

The skate save is initiated while the goaltender is in the standing position. It is used to stop pucks that are traveling directly on the ice surface or just an inch or so above it. The target of the puck is usually just next to the goalie between him and the uprights of the goal. It usually comes in on his stick side. If the puck is any higher than an inch or so off the ice, it can and should be stopped with the glove, blocker, or a pad. If it comes in on the glove side, it can either be snagged with the glove or stopped by the stick blade. By coming in low to the stick side, it is in a location that is very difficult for a goalie to defend against.

If a goalie moves to stop the puck using the stick, as the stick is moved toward the direction of the puck, it is often pulled up off the ice and the puck goes underneath it. If the pad is pushed over toward the puck, the puck is too low to hit the pad and goes underneath it. A goalie can try a butterfly stop, but if the puck is too close to his body and is headed close to the center line of the net, then it will go right between his legs. This is a highly effective location to shoot the puck if you are a scorer. The only viable option for the netminder is to attempt the skate save.

For purposes of illustration, we'll say the puck is coming in low to the stick or right side. To initiate the skate save, the goalie turns the right leg and pad 90 degrees directly right, pointing toward the goal upright. The skate blade remains flat against the ice surface. The goalie pushes the skate out toward the upright, sliding it along the ice and keeping the blade flat against the ice surface. In order to complete this action properly, the goalie must begin to go down to the ice by bending the left knee and kneeling with that knee on the ice. The blade of the right skate as it reaches the end of its travel will begin to pull up at the toe and will end on the heel. The secret to the skate save is to keep as much of the skate blade as possible flat against the ice surface for as long as possible so there is as much to contact the puck as possible. (See photo on page 146.)

A major disadvantage to this save is the enormous gap left between the goalie's legs. All attempts to completely cover this gap are fruitless. The goalie generally cannot protect it with the locker

This is a classic butterfly flop. The knees are in and the skates are out. It covers a lot of ice surface, but is difficult to recover from quickly.

The goalie has good form, keeping the skate blade flat on the ice to make the skate save.

and stick if he is on his left knee facing right, because the mitt and stick will be on the opposite side of the body inside the goal. It is difficult to protect it with the glove because the back of the hand will naturally face out toward the play with the pocket of the glove facing the inside of the leg. The best defense against this move is to pull the right leg in toward the center to close the gap as much as possible and to recover as quickly as possible back onto the skates and into the ready crouch for the next shot on goal.

Body Save

The body save seems to be made without the aid of any equipment. In reality, it is made with the equipment that is worn against the body under the jersey. This type of save is often a save of faith. The goalie must have faith that his equipment will keep the shot from hurting him and he must have faith in his ability to make the save. There is no classic style, no special maneuver to perform, no specific twisting angle. It is just a matter of getting the body in front of the puck to stop it from going into the goal.

A typical example of this type of save would be seen as follows. The goalie has just made a kick save toward the right side of the goal. The momentum of the kick has carried the netminder out a little further from the goal mouth then he would like to be. The puck rebounds to an opponent while the goalie is still down. There is no time to recover back to the ready crouch as the attacker has already fired the puck toward the opposite left side of the goal. The goalie lunges his body toward the opposite upright. Arms are outstretched and the body appears to be in full flight across the crease. The puck hits the goalie's chest just as the two arrive at the left post together. A goal is saved.

This is a good example of a body save. The goalie uses any part of his or her body that is available to stop the puck. Another good example of the use of the body save is when the puck is fired at about mid-chest height directly at the goalie. The goalie becomes unsure whether to stop the puck with the glove, blocker, or stick. It in essence "handcuffs" the goalie. The best stop in this case is to let the puck hit the chest, and then trap the puck against the chest and hold it for a stoppage of play.

The body save may also be used against difficult shots when stopping the puck with the upper arms, lower arms, or anything else. Again, the goalie must have faith the puck will not hurt and that it will be stopped. This is often a last resort type of save, but it still works. (See photo on page 148.)

One reason the goalie wears a lot of padding is that he will never know where the puck is going to hit him. This goalie is in no position to use his hands to stop a shot, so he made a great body save instead.

MISCELLANEOUS SITUATIONS

There are various situations a goaltender will encounter throughout the game of which he needs to be aware. Of course, the goalie also needs to know how to handle these special circumstances within the context of the game when they arise.

Dump-In

This is when the puck is leisurely dumped into the empty attack zone by the attacking team. The dump-in is generally employed when line changes occur during the play. The puck is usually not pursued except by a perfunctory player meant to harass the goalie. The goalie's best action here is to skate out to corral the puck around the face-off circles, look for a teammate entering the zone, and then shoot the puck quickly to the player (providing the opponent is not between the goalie and the teammate). The netminder doesn't want to hold onto the puck for a long time. He just does not have the stick-handling ability to keep it away from attackers for a long time. When in doubt about head-manning (shooting the puck up-ice to an open teammate), it is best to freeze the puck for a stoppage of play.

Wrap-Around

This is a dump-in that is fired hard and quickly along the side boards with the intention of getting the puck rapidly into the zone and around the rear boards possibly back up to an attacking teammate. The action of choice for the netminder is to stop the puck behind the net for a teammate to pick up. If the puck is fired somewhat slowly, the goaltender heads out of the crease toward the boards directly behind the net and waits for the puck to arrive to stop it.

If the puck is approaching with great speed, the goalie should head out around back of the net opposite the direction it is approaching and head for a point along the boards at the side and to the rear of the net. In this direction, the goalie will be facing the puck, can see it better as it is approaching, and have a better chance to stop it. Again, the netminder should leave the puck for a teammate to pick up. If no teammate is around, it is wisest to freeze the puck. (See photo on page 99.)

Icing

Because the goalie can best see the entire ice surface and consequently everyone on it, including the officials, the goalie can best tell his teammates when the officials are calling an icing. To inform his teammates that an icing call is on, so they do not injure themselves racing to the puck, the goalie should raise his catching glove straight into the air as soon as he sees that the official has called an icing.

Puck on the Net

The puck lodged on the back of the net is usually a call for a stoppage of play. Again, to inform teammates and the officials who may not be able to see the puck on the net, the goalie should raise his catching mitt straight up into the air and rapidly flick the wrist and glove down to indicate the puck is on the net. The official will quickly skate over behind the net and judge either that the play should continue or should be stopped.

Bouncing Puck

This is one of the hardest saves for a goalie to make. The direction of the puck bouncing about on its edge is nearly impossible to predict. If there is an incoming bouncing puck, the best play for the goalie is to skate out of the net as far as possible to meet the puck in a less dangerous zone of the ice; do not try to stop the puck with the stick or catch it with the glove. Get directly in front of the puck, get down on one knee, and attempt to trap the puck against the chest protector or leg pads. Use all of the body to stop the puck or at least knock the puck down to the ice. When the puck is stopped, immediately freeze the puck or clear it quickly to a teammate or the side boards.

The Fly Ball

Another play that is equally difficult for the goalie is to catch the flipped-in flying puck. Usually the goalie misplays the puck or loses it in the lights or against the dark ceiling of the rink. Like the procedure for the bouncing puck, he should skate out as far as feasible to meet it and use as much of his body as possible to stop it. Use of the basket catch is preferred. Keep the glove low and open upward directly in front of the chest. Use the other hand—the stick-mitt blocker pad—as a backup in case the puck bounces out of the glove. Again, once the goaltender is in control of the puck, it is his option what to do with it.

Breakaway

This is the most exciting and potentially dangerous goal-scoring opportunity in all of hockey. It is pure talent and exhilaration in motion. The first rule every goalie must remember is this: You are not going to stop them all! The second rule is similar to the first: On some shooters, you are not going to stop any. This situation is the least desirable that a goalie would choose.

The best action a netminder can take is to skate out to meet the attacker about ten to fifteen feet from the net. Skate directly out toward the skater. Do not make a move or show your intentions. Do not commit yourself in either direction or in any way if possible. As the skater moves toward you, back skate with the skater back toward the net, as always keeping yourself between the net and the shooter as much as possible. This is where patience and determination pay off. By not committing yourself, you are forcing the skater to make the first move. You can keep skating backward until the shooter runs out of net to shoot at and crosses the goal line. Remember, a goalie cannot anticipate what the shooter may do when the shooter doesn't know what he'll do himself. Only when the shooter shows his intentions should the goalie move to stop the puck. Use whatever save is quickest and most prudent at that time. The defense won't be far behind to handle any rebounds so don't worry about them. The important thing is to stop the initial shot.

To stop a breakaway is pure talent and a lot of luck. The only way to improve a goalie's breakaway reactions is to practice … practice … practice. A coach should always schedule time during practice in shooting drills to work on breakaways. The more confident a goalie is, the better he becomes. The better he becomes, the more confidence he'll have.

MISCELLANEOUS SKILLS, TASKS, AND ADDITIONAL CONTRIBUTIONS

The additional duties and responsibilities of the goaltender within the team and game setting have been touched on earlier. The goalie, although having the prime charge to stop the puck from going into the net, also is required to perform a number of equally important assignments to help the team win. Here is a short list of those chores and some accompanying information.

Cheerleader. The goalie is the team cheerleader. He should always be urging his team on and trying to bring up the spirits of his teammates.

Traffic Cop. It is the goaltender who generally directs traffic out of the zone. When the defense has turned the play up ice and the offense is shifting into position, it is the goaltender who should be calling out the location of his teammates and also the opponents on the ice his teammate's may not be able to see. The goalie is the one player who can usually see all the ice at once and who can help direct toward which side of the ice the play should be taken.

Timekeeper. Because the goalie can best see the game and penalty clocks while the play is at the other end of the rink, it is his duty to keep an eye on the clock, especially the penalty clock, and inform his teammates when the penalty is about to expire. This holds true for both penalty killing and man-advantage situations. Either goalie on the ice who is not involved in the play at the moment will usually slap his stick flat against the ice when there are about five seconds remaining on a penalty to let his team know that a man is about to leave the box.

Flow Breaker. More than any other player on the ice, it is the goaltender who can control the ebb and flow of the play and the game. If the netminder's team is getting too disorganized, then it is the duty of the goalie to stop the action to allow the team time to regroup. If the opponents are too organized and have excessive momentum, it is the job of the goalie to help break drive energy. This is accomplished through constant stoppages of play; by freezing the puck or simply by taking a few moment to adjust some equipment. Even if it takes just a few extra seconds to re-buckle a strap, those few seconds can be used to gather a breath or give teammates and coaches time to set strategy.

The Sixth Skater. Toward the end of the game with the team trailing by a goal, the coach may choose to "pull the goalie" in favor of a sixth attacker. The goalie needs to understand and accept his role in the situation, and be ready at the coach's signal to charge to the bench as fast as possible to get the extra skater on the ice. The goalie must also help set up the opportunity to get to the bench by stopping the puck, keeping the play alive and turning the puck up ice quickly so the defensive zone does not become filled with attackers.

GOALIE, NOT SCAPEGOAT

Coaches need to realize that goalies have feelings, too. Coaches cannot place the burden of loss square on the goalies' shoulders. The team as a unit plays the game and the team as a unit wins or loses the game. Coaches need to understand that the novice goalie is often a very scared youngster when starting out, that sometimes he might not really want to be in the nets, and that goalies are just as nervous as the rest of the players, especially about performing badly in a game.

When you tell your players to have fun out there, direct these comments to the goalies. Emphasize to them the importance of having fun. Remind them that it's just a game; the world doesn't revolve around who wins and who loses. If you have a good goalie, the knowledgeable hockey world (read: "scouts") can tell that even in a loss. Goalies seem to take the losses the hardest, so coaches have to work the hardest to make sure the youngsters don't feel the entire brunt of the loss.

WRAP-UP

Employing the above principles and exercises, the goalie will in no time be a candidate for the Vezina trophy. It is up to the goalie how much time and effort to devote to the "goal" of improving skills. In every position, the longer and more often a player plays, the better he becomes. This is certainly true in goaltending. Encourage your netminders to play at every opportunity. Your whole team will be pleased with the improved play.

Well, you finally have a team together ready to play. The skills are practiced; the plays are memorized; the uniforms and equipment are in place. Your team is ready to take the ice for the first game and—hopefully—victory. Hold on! Not so fast! There are still just a few more details we need to cover before the referee drops the puck for the opening face-off. Turn to the next chapter to find out how not to be embarrassed as a team in your first game.

7.

PLAYING THE GAME

One thing needs to be made clear to the team from the start. The coach has the final say in all matters concerning the team and its function on the ice. Assistant coaches and team captains can have their say, but when the coach stands to talk, all should fall silent.

At the pre-game meeting, you, as coach, will go over the line matches and makeup, review the defensive partners, and, most importantly, discuss final game strategy. No excuses are accepted if a player misses this meeting. I assemble lines with the players. I then assign each line a number, usually 1 through 4, and announce the line constructions and their assigned numbers. I do the same for the defensive pairings. During the game, this makes it easy to call out lines for changes and to tell which players have just come off the ice and who needs ice time next. I make sure my "top" line is not always line number one. This makes each child feel special. They know that they will be the prized "starters" in the game when they are assigned to line number one.

The coach will also give the pre-game pep talk. This does not need to be the "rah-rah" type of speech heard in the movies. I usually just remind the players of their assignments and to focus on the game. I emphasize positive thinking and fair play. Finally, I tell my team to *Have fun out there*! Enjoy yourself! Play the game. Don't play each other and don't play the opponents. If you stick to the game plan and don't panic, all will come out all right." Then I send them on their merry way to the ice charged up for a victory.

Before your team actually hits the ice for the first game, there are a few other equally important points that need to be covered.

At some point before the first game, your team will need to either elect or assign a team captain and two assistant captains. There are a few things to keep in mind. If the players elect a captain in an open vote, a popular player usually will be elected. This player may not always be the best leadership choice for the team. Players who join the team in groups have a tendency to stick together, and the larger or more influential of the groups may elect one of their own, not giving a truly appropriate player the opportunity to lead. An elected captain who is not deserving of the honor may divide players instead of uniting them.

CAPTAINS

The captain should be a player who leads by example. He should know how to motivate the other players and not be afraid to stand up and speak out when things are going wrong. As the coach, you need a captain who can work with you and the rest of the team. You need someone who doesn't always gripe and complain, who can carry out assignments without fail.

Over the years I have come up with a compromise that provides the team with a choice while ensuring the quality of the captain. For the first few games I assign three assistant captains and select one of these to be the captain designate for a game. I confer with the players before I announce their names to see if they are willing to accept the responsibility. I try to choose a player from each of any existing cliques and to choose players who have demonstrated leadership during practice sessions. I may keep the same three players as assistant captains for each game or may change them according to how games go and who shows up to play them.

If things go well, I then let the team vote from these assistant captains. I have not thrust any player into the spotlight who does not want to be there, I have given a player the opportunity to experience the captaincy even if only for one game, and I have shown the team that other players may be equally qualified. However, if things are not going well and I feel there is time for a change, I can always change the captains. I make sure that the team—and the captain—realize I am not blaming the captains for the problems. More than likely it is my fault, anyway. No, I am changing just for the sake of a change; just to shake things up a bit.

TAKING THE ICE

Well, now you have a team, and it's time to take the ice. Have your starting goaltender lead the team out onto the ice and let's go!

Warm-Up

As your team hits the ice for the first time, it's best to have your players skate counter-clockwise around the rink for a few laps to "get their legs." The mental preparation has already taken place in the locker room. During these laps, the players should be stretching out their bodies to prepare for the game. They should be wearing all of their equipment. Each player should be performing the following exercises as they skate around the ice. You may choose to have your captain lead the exercises.

ARM AND BACK STRETCH

Place the stick crosswise behind the back just below the neck around the shoulder blade. Hook each arm forward over the shaft of the stick. As the player is skating, he should twist at the waist and turn the stick in half turns in helicopter fashion in order to stretch the back and waist muscles. Also have them bend down at the waist or tilt back slightly and repeat the procedure. The players also can place the stick around the lower back and twist and turn as described. These should continue for about a half lap.

KNEE BENDS

While skating, hold the stick with both hands straight out in front of the body parallel to the ice and horizontal to the body. Bend deep at the knees and go up and down slowly for a few yards. Then, skating on one blade, bend the opposite leg and pull the knee up toward the chest. Hook the stick around and under the knee cap and pull inward. Repeat for the other leg. Finally, go down in the knee bends again, and alternatively push the legs out behind with toes pointing out (not down) and let each drag for a few yards. This stretches the ligaments and muscles sideways on the trailing leg.

LEG KICKS

While skating, hold the stick horizontally in both hands out in front of the chest with arms extended. Simply kick out a leg repeatedly in front as though trying to kick the stick. Change legs and repeat. This builds stability and balance.

SKATING

Skate around the rink at varying speeds. Go fast, then slow, skate around the rink both forward and backward. At each line, both red and blue, the players should alternate between forward skating and backward skating. Players should pivot on one foot at each line alternating forward and backward, left and right.

During this time, the coach should be watching for any players who appear hurt or injured. After about five minutes of skating, the coach or captain should begin to throw practice pucks onto the ice in the direction of the goal. This is a signal to the players they should begin shooting and warming-up the goaltenders.

At this time, the captain organizes the players into two lines at the center of the blue line with right-hand shooters on the right and left-hand shooters on the left. The captain, off to one side, takes one puck at a time and shoots it toward center ice where two players — one from the right and one from the left line — are breaking toward the goal. The two players then attack the goal, passing the puck back and forth, on a close-in breakaway.

After a few minutes of this activity, the captain then calls for the two lines to separate from each other on opposite sides of the ice. The captain again shoots the loose pucks alternating to each line. The players then break in on goal one at a time and shoot on the goal from near the slot area.

Finally, the captain calls for the entire team to spread across the blue line. Each player has a puck. In rapid-fire fashion, each player from either left to right or alternating right then left fires the puck toward the goal. If there are not enough pucks for the entire team, perform the procedure in waves with as many pucks as you have. During these three activities, it is best to have the goalies alternate in goal every few minutes so each goaltender is equally warmed up.

These are not the only things a team can do to warm up, but they can get you started. A coach may be aware of an area in which the team needs some extra work and may want to emphasize this in warmup. This will be among the last things your team works on just before the game and will be freshest in their memories.

The referee usually lets the teams warm up for about ten minutes. All these activities will have to be completed in that time.

When the referee blows the whistle, urge your team to quickly gather the pucks and crowd around you for last minute instructions. While your team is warming up, you or one of your assistant coaches should watch the other team, especially their goaltender. This scouting should spot any weaknesses or poor tendencies on the part of the individual opposing players and their team as a whole. At the final team meeting just before the face-off, you may want to stress to the team to do certain things. For example, you may stress to shoot high to the opposing goalie's glove side because he always goes down automatically on long shots or you may instruct them to take booming slapshots because he flinches on them. Use the scouting information to your team's advantage.

After some final instructions, it's time for a team cheer. It may sound corny, but it isn't. It's a chance for all the players and coaches to get together for final encouragement and support. Even something as simple as "One-two-three ... let's go now!" works. After that, the starting line-up skates into position and the rest of the team sits on the bench.

THE GAME

Even how your team sits on the bench is important. The defensemen should be sitting next to their defensive partners on the defensive end of the bench. That is, if the team is defending the goal to the right, then the defensemen should sit down on the right end of the bench. Conversely, the offensive lines should be sitting together on the offensive end of the bench. Each period, the players will be sitting on different ends of the bench. This provides the most efficient preliminary procedure to change lines. When there are whole line changes (all five players), the players do not cross one other on the ice while getting off nor do they bump into other players disrupting the line shift. Also, as the players come off the bench, they are closest to their playing positions. They don't have to skate those few extra yards to get into position.

Line Changes

With really little players, some leagues require the referee to blow the whistle for a line change every two to three minutes, regardless of activity on the ice. This is so each player gets equal time while it teaches the concept of team play and line changes. It emphasizes the point that one player does not play the whole game. Also, little players have a hard time getting over the boards. If your league does not do this, or your team is older, line changes are accomplished in a different manner.

Hockey is an unusual sport in that it permits player substitution while play is active. Although this procedure is very exciting and keeps the play alive, it can also be disastrous to many teams. Numerous teams get caught in line changes that result in a goal or at least a good scoring chance for the opponents.

Well before the next line change is due, the coach should have called out the next line or line number to hit the ice. Usually I follow a numerical progression from one to four, so the players automatically know who will be next. There are occasions when I want to switch line match-ups against the other team, so I'll call out a different number. I may need to shift lines periodically during the period to match a particular player against a specific opposing player. Also, if there are power plays or man-short situations, the lines will juggle significantly. If this is done with any regularity, I'll change line numbers or line combinations between periods to match what I want. I may even assign "specialty team" line numbers so all players get a chance on the special units. Generally, the lines remain the same throughout the entire game.

Optimally, the team will change lines when a whistle blows and there is no need to rush in and out of the box. But that doesn't always occur and the lines must change "on the fly." First, I make it known that everyone on the bench in uniform must sit between their shifts. The coaches need the organization to see who is available to talk to and who is ready to go. The line ready to go onto the ice will stand up only when called. This is a signal to the line on the ice that they need to come off when they get a chance. The line standing will also call out loudly "change ... change" to the ice.

The best time to make a line change is on a dump-in. The player carrying the puck should just skate across the red line to avoid an icing, and then dump the puck into the offensive corner opposite the player box. This gives the whole team the opportunity to change easily, and keeps the opposing team on the ice as they need to go back and corral the puck. By the time the other team has regained the puck, the next line should be on the ice attacking the zone.

But a dump-in is not always possible, nor is it always possible to change the whole line at once. There will be times when you'll need to change lines one player at a time. As one of the players on the ice is away from the play, and each should make it his responsibility to get away from the play at an opportune time, he skates over toward the bench and loudly calls out his line position such as center, left wing, right wing, left defense, or right defense. When he is within five feet of the bench and not involved in the play, the player taking the ice jumps over the boards and the player entering the box enters near his team's end of the ice through the end door which is being opened by either the non-playing goaltender or an assistant coach or trainer. Of course, in extreme situations, they can enter through either door or simply fall over the boards just to get in quickly. The line should sit together on the bench so one of the coaches can discuss with the line as a whole what just happened on the ice and what to do next shift.

The players going over the boards also need to go over in a way that will not injure themselves or their teammates. The player should turn slightly with his back to the ice, sit on top of the boards, and then pull and lift his legs over the boards with the skates hugging the boards. Any other way is too dangerous to the other players sitting on the bench with skates flying in all directions. In addition, skates have a tendency to get tangled in each other when players try to get out onto the ice via their own methods. Stick to the proven method.

PENALTIES

Inevitably, one of your players will get a penalty. I stress to my players *never, ever* argue with the referees. It's not sportsmanlike. The player may think that the refs are wrong, but he must go to the box anyway. I do tell my players they may ask the referee what they did wrong and how they might correct or avoid it next time, but do it after the play has stopped or between periods. Penalties should serve as a learning experience for the player.

When in the penalty box, the player should be in constant visual contact with the bench. The coach may want the player to return immediately to the ice or head directly over to the bench to be replaced on the ice. It is the coach's job to clearly communicate his intention to the player in the penalty box. If not, the team may end up with a penalty for having too many men on the ice.

Most of the time in junior hockey, there are no penalty box timekeepers. As mentioned above, the goalie should be assisting the player in knowing when the penalty is up. Ultimately, however, it is the player's responsibility to watch the clock and come out of the box on time. Make sure your players know to come over the boards exactly as the penalty expires. Referees often keep an eye on this situation and will assess another penalty for leaving the box too early. Also, players shouldn't "go to sleep" in the box. I've seen players serve much longer than their necessary time because they weren't mentally in the game. Tell your players: "Stay awake out there" or in this case, "in there!"

BETWEEN PERIODS

In junior hockey, teams very rarely get more than a few minutes between periods. Usually the teams don't even bother going to the locker room. I have my players gather around the player's bench and sit and relax. It provides a few minutes that I can use to talk to my players while they are all assembled. It is a time to make minor adjustments to lines or positions or even some plays.

The players are often tired and prefer to just listen, and that's the way it should be. The coach should have the undivided attention of every member of the team. It is not a time to argue, fight, or even discuss; it is a time to listen and then act.

AFTER THE GAME

Win or lose, I emphasize it again to my team, "Have fun!" It's just a game. It really is just children putting in a few hours of fun (and improving themselves at the same time). When the game is over, we're all back to being children, regardless of age. No grudges, no fights, no complaining. I send my players out onto the ice as a team to shake hands with the other players.

To me, this is the most wonderful tradition in any sport. After the game is over, each team should line up in single file at center ice and skate past the other team shaking hands. It lets the players

After the game, players and coaches alike line up at center ice to offer their congratulations or support to their opponents.

know that no matter what the differences between the two teams are on the ice, all is forgotten after the game is over.

In the locker room after the game, the coach should talk to the players objectively about their efforts. Praise the good efforts; the hustles and the good plays. Point out the lack of concentration on certain plays. The coach should make notes about what was discussed so as to know what to work on in the next practice. The coach needs to stay both optimistic and realistic. These players are not professionals. They are just kids out to have a good time and it is essential you remember that.

The players want nothing more than to just get out of there. They're tired and hungry, and they might even have some unfinished schoolwork to do. They don't really want to listen to you at this time. Now, however, is the time to talk. By discussing the small things now, you keep them fresh in the player's minds for the next practice. After you've had your say, ask if anyone else wants to talk. If not, remind them of the next practice and send them home.

Congratulations, coach! You have just completed your first game! You have created a team from a diverse group of kids; some rag-tag, some enthusiastic, some apprehensive, some egotistical. You have boys and girls who *really* want to play hockey. You have given them the opportunity to prove to themselves, to their parents, and to you that they can play as a team.

Good luck in the rest of your games. Regardless of the outcome, you deserve a standing ovation. You have earned it.

GLOSSARY

Hockey has its own set of highly specialized terms and phrases. These aren't confusing unless you're new to the game, then they can cause some problems. Here is a comprehensive list of terms that will serve to help the coach speak the lingo. If nothing else, you at least will sound as though you know what you're doing.

ALUMINUM SHAFT—A stick shaft made of hollow aluminum. The wooden blade is totally detachable from the shaft, making it easy to switch broken blades while keeping the same flex and torsion in the shaft. This helps cut down on stick maintenance time. Sticks with aluminum shafts are very expensive.

ASSISTANT CAPTAIN—One of three team leaders elected or chosen by the team or coaches. The assistants fill in for the captain and assume the captaincy responsibilities and duties when he is not present at the game or on the ice. The captain and the assistants are the only players permitted to speak with the referee concerning the rules when there is a dispute on the ice.

ATHLETIC PROTECTOR—Also referred to as the "cup." A highly protective and padded piece of equipment designed to fit over and around the crotch and groin area of male players to protect against impact injury.

ATTACK ZONE—The area between the blue line and the red goal line as a team is attacking the opposing goal. Most goals are scored from this zone, and control of the zone is essential in controlling and winning a game.

BACK-CHECK—Checking actions taken by the forward line of a team in their own defensive zone against opposing forwards to regain control of the puck from an attacking team. Back-checking counteracts fore-checking and helps prevent goals.

BACKHAND PASS—A pass made with the convex back portion of the stick. The stick (and eventually the puck on it) is pulled back with the lower hand in the direction of intended travel. The puck should travel along or very close to the ice with little or no follow-through.

BACKHAND SHOT—Like the backhand pass but made more forcefully, usually toward the goal in an attempt to score. The shot may be lifted high toward the goal with a high follow-through and a quick flip.

BLOCKER MITT—Also known as the stick mitt or waffle mitt. A large, leather-covered, rectangular piece of thick plastic attached to the back of a leather glove worn on the goalie's stick-holding hand. Used to prevent injury to the back of the hand and also to help deflect shots away from the net. A very effective piece of equipment used to stop a number of very difficult shots.

BLOCKER SAVE—An attempt by the goaltender to stop a fired puck with the blocker mitt. A highly directable save that produces a substantial rebound.

BOARDS—The walls that completely surround the skating ice surface.

BODY CHECK—see CHECK.

BODY SAVE—A save made by the goaltender with any part of the body in any possible fashion to prevent the puck from entering the net.

BREAKAWAY—Usually, an opponent skating in with the puck on an undefended goaltender in the attack zone. There are no other forwards or defensemen from either team accompanying the skater or helping the goalie defend the goal. There are also two-on-one or three-on-one breakaways.

CAPTAIN—A player from the team elected by his or her peers or chosen by the coach to lead the team on the ice. The responsibilities of the captain include, but are not limited to: speaking with the referee concerning the rules, leading the team in practice, conducting team meetings, acting as a cheerleader, and acting as a liaison between the coach and the team.

CATCHING GLOVE—See CATCHING MITT.

CATCHING MITT—Also known as the glove mitt or the catching glove on the goaltender, it resembles a first baseman's mitt in baseball. It is used primarily to catch a puck that is still in flight.

CHECK—The use of the body to hit the puck carrier in a pushing, shoving, or knocking action in an attempt to make the puck carrier lose control of the puck. The action is legal only against the puck carrier or a player in the immediate vicinity of the puck.

CRADLING — A movement performed by a player on the ice while carrying the puck with the stick. The player keeps the puck nestled inside the curve of the stick to protect it from opponents and to move it around the ice.

CRASH THE NET—The act of one, two, or all three members of an offensive line skating directly and sharply in toward the opposing net to overflow the offensive zone to confuse the defense. This is used primarily to set up deflection shots from the point or to pick up rebounds for a scoring attempt.

CREASE—The shaded, semi-circular area directly in front of the net delineated by a red line on the ice, with a radius of approximately five feet. It is considered off limits to all players except for the goaltender at all times unless the puck is in it.

CROSS-ICE PASS — A pass made between two teammates that crosses untouched over the center passing lane on the ice. Usually made from boards to boards in an attempt to free a player for a breakaway.

CROSS-OVER—A turn in which the outside skate is lifted high off the ice, crossed over the inside skate, and planted on the other side of the inside skate. This is the fastest and most efficient way to make a turn.

CUTTING DOWN THE ANGLE—A defense used by the goalie against a breakaway where the goalie moves out of the crease and approaches the puck carrier. By moving out of the crease toward the shooter, the goaltender presents a more obstructed view of the net and thus leaves less of the net visible for the shooter to shoot toward.

DEFENSEMEN—The two players on the ice directly in front of the goaltender who help protect the goal and help prevent pucks from going into the net. It is not their job to stop the puck, but to help prevent the shots that produce goals. Defensemen also clear away any rebounds or opposing players standing in the vicinity of the net who may pick up rebounds.

DEFENSIVE BOX—When in a penalty or man short situation, the team's four remaining skaters form a box in the defensive zone in front of the goal to help protect it. The box consists of two forwards at the upper or point positions and two defensemen back near the goal. The box then operates as a unit to keep players and the puck out of scoring areas.

DEFENSIVE PARTNERS—Two defensemen paired together on a regular basis, usually one with a left-hand shot and the other with a right-hand shot. The defensive partners have predetermined assignments and know who will cover what positions or players in any given situation.

DEFLECTION—When the puck is redirected from its original flight path toward the goal by a stick, leg, skate, or any other means. Because of its spontaneous flight path, it is very difficult to anticipate and defend against.

DEKE—The act of feigning intentions with the puck.

DRAG STOP—A skating stop in which the player drags his trailing skate along the ice at an angle perpendicular to the direction of travel to slow his speed.

DROP PASS—The action of leaving the puck behind on the ice for a trailing player, hopefully a teammate, to pick up.

DUMP-IN—A controlled shot to no-one or nothing in particular where the puck is shot from just over and inside the red line into the opposing offensive corner. Used primarily to set up a line change or to turn the defending players back quickly into their own zone in order to set up an offensive attack.

FACE GUARD—A coated wire cage or plastic shield that completely covers and protects the face. The guard attaches to the helmet at the forehead and secures with a chin strap. Required for play at all amateur levels of hockey.

FACE MASK—Similar to the face guard but worn by the goaltender. Often slightly modified for increased protection. Must be approved for competitive play by the Canadian Standards Association as capable of withstanding certain forces. Required for play at all amateur levels.

FACE SHIELD—A face guard that is usually only half length covering the face from the eyes down to the nose area. These are never approved for play in organized amateur competitive play due to the areas of the face below the nose that remain unprotected.

FACE-OFF—The action of the referee dropping the puck fairly between two opposing waiting centers to put the puck into play to begin play action.

FACE-OFF CIRCLE—Any of the five areas on the ice in which most face-offs will occur. They are surrounded by a painted circle to outline the protective areas into which other players may not enter.

FAST START—A type of running, almost jumping, skating start to give a player a quick jump into the play. Although it takes significant exertion on the player's part, it gets him into the action quickly.

FIVE HOLE—On a goaltender in a normal goalie crouch, it is the small, triangular area between the leg pads just below the crotch and above the stick blade into which pucks can be hit. It is a very vulnerable area on a goalie as it is very difficult to defend against. It is a favorite target area for shooters.

FLAT GROUND—The very bottom of a goaltender's skate blade that is solid and flat with perpendicular sides to give the goaltender maximum skate area on the ice surface for maximum stability.

FLIP PASS—A flat, short, quick pass to a teammate produced by a flick of the wrist to get the puck just off the ice surface and over any possible low obstructions.

FOLLOW-THROUGH — The act of moving the stick up and through the path of the puck after the shot has been taken. In most cases, the player should not stop the motion of the stick swing as the stick contacts the puck, but should continue moving the stick up and through the initially intended path of the puck. Usually, the higher the follow-through, the higher off the ice the puck will go.

FORE-CHECK—An action by the attacking team of checking the defensive team in the offensive zone in an attempt to gain or regain possession of the puck to establish a scoring chance. Fore-checking is most effective in the corners and in front of the net.

FOREHAND PASS—A pass of the puck made with the stick in the usual hand positions with the puck on the front of the stick inside the curve of the blade.

FORWARD—Any of the three players comprising a line who initiate most of the scoring opportunities. They are the center, the left wing, and the right wing.

FREEZE THE PUCK—The action of stopping, holding, or preventing the puck from moving in any direction, causing the referee to blow the whistle to stop play. Used most effectively when a team is disorganized and is trying to regroup or regain composure. When employed by a player without cause, a player risks having a "delay of game" penalty called on him. Play resumes with a face-off.

GLOVE MITT—See CATCHING MITT.

GLOVE SAVE—The action by the goalie of stopping the puck from going into the net by using the glove mitt.

GOAL MOUTH—The six by four foot opening of the net.

GOALTENDER (also GOALIE, GOALKEEPER, KEEP, NETMINDER)—The player charged with the responsibility of preventing the puck from going into the net.

HEAD-MANNING — The act of pushing or shooting the puck quickly up ice to a breaking or skating teammate to quickly formulate an offensive play.

HOCKEY GLOVES — Special, highly protective gloves that a skater uses to hold the stick. Unlike other gloves, the fingers do not wrap around the stick shaft but rather hold it claw- or pincer-like.

HOCKEY STOP—Stopping a skating stride on the ice by turning both skates parallel with the toes in the same direction and digging the skate blade edges into the ice while gliding across it. This is a fast and safe stop that a player can use to change direction quickly.

HOLLOW GROUND — The very narrow and concave surface running the length of a skater's blades, essentially giving each blade two edges. These two edges give skaters' advantages when stopping and turning.

ICING—The action of shooting the puck from the opposite side of the red line down the ice across the red, blue, and goal lines into the offensive zone. This is an illegal action and play will stop immediately in amateur hockey.

INSIDE EDGE—On hollow ground blades, the two edges of the skate blades that are closest to each other on the inside of the skates.

KEEP—Shortened version of GOALKEEPER.

KICK SAVE—A save employed by the goalie, involving kicking his leg pad toward the puck to prevent it from entering the net. The kick save results in the goalie doing the splits and landing in a poor position to quickly stop any subsequent shots.

KILLING A PENALTY—A term used to describe a team with a player in the penalty box.

LATERAL SLIDE—The act of sliding sideways across the ice. Used by the goalie as he slides across the goal crease from one side to the other, keeping the pads square to the play.

LEAD PASS—The act of passing the puck to a teammate who is

ahead of the puck carrier on the ice. The puck passer attempts to pass the puck slightly ahead of the puck receiver so that the puck receiver does not have to break stride or slow down in order to gain control of the puck.

LEADING THE SKATER—Anticipating the receiving skater's future location when making a pass. When the passer passes the puck to the receiver's future location rather than his location upon initiation of the pass. This is most important when making a cross-ice pass.

LEFT-HANDED SHOT—A shot that has both the puck and the stick on the left side of the shooter's body.

LEG PADS—The big, thick, heavy pads worn by the goaltender on his legs. Used to stop the majority of the pucks shot toward the net.

LIFT PASS—See FLIP PASS.

LINE—Three teammates playing together as one offensive unit. A line consists of one center, one left wing, and one right wing. May occasionally be used to refer to the defensive pairing as a defensive line.

LINE CHANGE—When either the offensive or defensive lines need to come off the ice due to fatigue and a new line enters the ice to continue the play. Play does not necessarily stop when a line change takes place as it can be performed "on the fly."

MAN ADVANTAGE—When a team has one player serving time in the penalty box and the opposing team has one more player on the ice. The team with the additional player is considered to have the man advantage.

MAN SHORT—A team having one player in the penalty box leaving the opposing team with one more player on the ice. This team is considered to be a "man short" for the length of the penalty.

NEUTRAL ZONE CHECKING — Checking the puckhandler when the puck is between the two blue lines. It is an attempt by either team to gain control of the puck.

OFF-ICE OFFICIAL—A game official assigned by the home team to take care of the administrative responsibilities of the game. These officials include timekeepers, penalty box attendants, shot keepers, and official scorers.

OFF WING—The wing opposite the normal position of a wing. For example, the right wing may occasionally be required to play left wing. This would put him in his off wing.

OFFENSIVE LINE—see LINE.

OFFSET PENALTY—When a player from each team is serving penalty time neither team plays a man short. Both teams play with a a full squad of players for the length of the penalty. The players may not return to the ice until the first stoppage of play after the penalty time has expired.

OFFSIDES—When any offensive player precedes the puck across the blue line into the offensive zone.

ON THE FLY—See LINE CHANGE.

ONE-TIMER—A shot taken by a player immediately as the puck slides in front of him. The shooter does not waste time setting up the shot or attempting to get closer in; he is poised for the shot as the puck goes in front of him.

OPEN MAN—A skater who is not being guarded by an opposing player.

OPEN NET—When the net is not being guarded by the goaltender.

OUTSIDE EDGE—On hollow ground blades, the two edges of the skate blades that are furthest from each other on the outside of the skates.

PAD SAVE—A save made by the goaltender with any part of the leg pad.

PASS—To transfer control of the puck from the puck carrier to a teammate.

PENALTY—Playing time served in the penalty box by a player for an infraction of the rules of the game. The team may play a man short, or the penalties may be offsetting. In either instance, the time is charged to the individual player. Accumulation of too many minutes or number of penalties may lead to game expulsion or the player may be suspended for the next game.

PENALTY BOX—A closed off and isolated area across the ice from the player boxes, next to the scorer's desk, in which players must serve the penalty time assessed to them.

POINT—During a sustained offensive attack, either of the two outer areas of the attack zone near the blue line just out from the boards manned by players who usually have very good slapshots. The players who control the point control the flow of the game.

POWER PLAY—When a team is assessed a penalty and must play a man short, the opposing team is said to have a power play for the length of the penalty.

PRE-GAME MEETING—A short but intense meeting held just before the team takes the ice. At the meeting, the coach will review the line configurations, the line match-ups, and strategy for the game and give the team last minute words of encouragement.

PUBLIC HOCKEY—An open ice skating session held at the local rink where anyone can go and play hockey for a few hours for a few dollars. Check local rink for rules and regulations regarding proper equipment.

PUCK—The one inch by three inch circular piece of vulcanized rubber that every one wants on their stick, but not in their face. The pucks are frozen rock hard before each game so they won't bounce around on the ice.

PULL THE GOALIE—When a team is down by one or two goals at the end of the game, with only a minute or so remaining on the clock, the coach may choose to remove the goalie from the net and replace him on the ice with a sixth skater, usually a forward, for added offensive attack. At this point in the game, it doesn't matter if the team loses by three goals or four goals, you still lose, but the opportunity to score a tying goal is greatly increased.

PURE SHOOTERS—Players who prefer to do nothing except get the puck and shoot for goals.

REBOUND — When the puck bounces back into the offensive zone directly in front of the net after a successful save by the goaltender. A large number of goals are scored by players who control the rebounds.

RIGHT-HANDED SHOT—A shot that has both the puck and the stick on the right side of the shooter's body.

ROCKER CUT — The shape into which a forward's or defenseman's skate blade is ground or sharpened. When held against a flat hard surface, the skate will rock on the blade from toe to heel. The more rocker cut on a blade, the less blade there is on the ice at any given time. Forwards generally have more of a rocker cut to give them higher flexibility in turning on the ice, while defenseman have less of a rocker cut to give them more stability.

SCREEN—The act of getting in front of the goaltender while play is in motion to block his view of the play. If a goalie is unable to see the puck or the player shooting it, he will be less likely to stop it.

SHADOW—The act of closely guarding one specific player from the opposite team or the name for the offensive player doing the shadowing. The shadow harasses the opponent to make it difficult for him to become actively involved in the play.

SHOVEL PASS—A pass that involves pushing the puck along the ice with the bottom edge of the stick blade. Primarily used to move the puck along the ice a short distance rather than to attempt to score.

SKATE SAVE—A save made by the goaltender with the skate blade or boot of the skate. This save is generally made in the lower corners of the net with the skate blades flat on the ice or slightly tilted up.

SLAPSHOT—A fast and hard shot that involves drawing the stick back high above the shoulder, then pulling down and driving through the puck with full force and high follow-through to give the puck maximum power and speed.

SLIDE SHOT—A variation of the shovel pass made with purpose, direction, and effort either toward a teammate or toward the goal in an attempt to score a goal.

SLOT—The area directly in front of the goal crease between the face-off circles, approximately ten feet wide and fifteen feet long. This is a prime area from which to score and the team controlling the slot usually controls the play.

SNAPSHOT—A half or quarter slapshot made similarly but with the stick coming back only one half or one quarter of the distance of the slapshot. This shot will transfer reduced power to the puck but allow the player to maintain significant speed.

SNOWPLOW STOP—The act of stopping by turning both skate blades inward up to forty-five degrees at the toes, and pressing down with the toes to the ice. It is a slow and labored stop but keeps the body stable on the ice and square to the play.

SOFT HANDS—The ability to score delicately. Said of the player who is very agile at stick-handling while carrying the puck and is able to perform a wide range of tricky maneuvers with the puck especially when around the net.

SPECIALTY TEAM—A squad or line of players on the team that has the primary responsibility to be out on either the power play or in man-short situations. The lines practice specific plays designed to maximize the situation.

SPLITS—The action of the goaltender when he goes down to the ice to make a kick save. One leg is split out right and the other is split out left. This is a very difficult position to recover from and makes the goaltender very vulnerable.

STAGGERED—When an offensive line enters the attack zone, they should not cross the blue line three abreast but staggered, with the puck carrier leading the other two players across the line.

STICK BLADE—The wide, flat, and sometimes curved wooden part of the stick at the very bottom of the shaft. The puck is shot and passed with the stick blade.

STICK CHECK—An attempt by one player to use the stick blade in a swinging, pushing, or shoving motion to knock the puck off an opponent's stick. If it is performed too aggressively, or not close enough to the puck, the player may be called for a "slashing" penalty.

STICK MITT—See BLOCKER MITT.

STICK SAVE—A save made by the goaltender using the stick to stop the puck.

STICK SHAFT—The long thin handle of the stick. While made of wood on most sticks, it can also be made of hollow aluminum. See also ALUMINUM SHAFT.

TAPE—Usually white cloth medical tape or black cloth electrical tape that is wrapped around the stick blade a few turns to help control the puck and hide it from opponents.

TIP-IN—To place the stick blade in the path of an incoming puck in an attempt to deflect it and redirect it toward the goal.

TOE SAVE—A save made by the goaltender with the tip of the outstretched skate.

TRAILING—The act of following the play, but not being directly involved in or up with the play.

VEZINA TROPHY—The trophy for the best goaltender in the National Hockey League.

WAFFLE—See BLOCKER MITT.

WARM-UP—The five to ten minute session just before the start of the game where the players stretch their muscles, get their skating legs, and help the goaltender prepare for the game.

WOODEN SHAFT—A stick shaft made from wood. The wooden shaft is permanently attached to the stick blade and the entire stick must be discarded if any part of the stick is broken.

WRAP-AROUND—A hard shot into the attack zone along the boards and glass. The momentum of the shot wraps the puck around behind the goal and into the opposite corner where it is often met by another player to begin a play.

WRIST SHOT—A quick, fast shot using wrist strength to snap the puck toward the goal. Usually taken where there is no room for wind-up or stick pull-back.

ZAMBONI—The machine that cleans the ice surface between periods and after games.

ZONE—Any of the three areas on the ice separated by the two blue lines. There is an attack zone, a neutral zone, and a defensive zone. Each zone is named in relation to a particular team and how it views the ice during any particular period.

ZONE CLEARS—Pucks shot from one end of the ice to the other in an attempt to dump the puck out of the zone quickly.

INDEX

A complete catalog of Betterway Books is available FREE by writing to the address shown below, or by calling toll-free 1-800-289-0963. To order additional copies of this book, send in retail price of the book plus $3.00 postage and handling for one book, and $1.00 for each additional book. Ohio residents add 5½% sales tax. Allow 30 days for delivery.

Betterway Books
1507 Dana Avenue
Cincinnati, Ohio 45207

Stock is limited on some titles; prices subject to change without notice.